THE WEIMAR INSANITY

Photographs and Propaganda from the Nazi Era

Stanley,

With best wishes,

Christopher Hill.

12th Sept. 1999.

THE WEIMAR INSANITY

Photographs and Propaganda from the Nazi Era

Christopher Hurndall

*An illustrated account of the birth of the Nazi
Party and the rise of Adolf Hitler to power.
Incorporating original photographs and
propaganda material translated from Nazi
Party journals of the period by Renate
Hurndall.*

The Book Guild Ltd
Sussex, England

The Book Guild Ltd.
25 High Street,
Lewes, Sussex

First published 1996
© Christopher Hurndall

Typesetting by Acorn Bookwork, Salisbury, Wiltshire

Printed in Great Britain by
Bookcraft (Bath) Ltd, Avon

A catalogue record for this book is
available from the British Library

ISBN 1 85776 111 1

CONTENTS

To our dear friends,
without whose magnificent support
this work could never have been published

LIST OF ILLUSTRATIONS

My name, that by my own perseverence I have attained, is my title.

Adolf Hitler
Siemenstadt, November 1933

INTRODUCTION

One of my earliest recollections as a young boy was in September 1945, accompanying my parents to see Noël Coward's play *Sigh No More* at the Piccadilly Theatre in London. The significance of the title, let alone the production itself, was way over my head, but what I do remember well were the open-topped buses with those outside staircases, the electric trams, the little blue taxis with spoked wheels, and all full of happy, jovial people.

Germany had surrendered exactly four months earlier, but Japan too had finally capitulated, and everyone seemed overjoyed at the news and the prospect of peace at last. My father's diary, which I have before me, reads: '*May 8th 1945, Tuesday, Moscow.* [He was serving at the time as head of the British Military Mission in Russia.] *V.E. Day. Well it's all over, Germany has surrendered, and may we prove worthy of the victory.*' He goes on to say: '*Everyone at the Embassy assembled at 4pm to hear the Prime-minister speak on this most historic occasion. In the evening we all gathered again to listen to the King, and the embassy party went on till late!*' Today, half of the world's population would not have been alive at the time, yet, had victory swung the other way, I wonder how many would have been born at all. Time heals so quickly, it's frightening.

Not long after our evening with Noël Coward, my father was recalled to duty and sent out to Hannover, where he joined the staff of the Control Commission of Germany, the British administrative authority set up soon after the war and tasked with the responsibility for operational and logistic control of the British Zone of occupation. His first 12 months there would doubtless fill a book on its own, for his diary is full of praise for the British Government in its efforts to rebuild the German nation, yet at the same time is scathing about some of the highly unsuitable individuals chosen to carry out this very important work.

Some 14 months later, on 22 November 1946 to be exact, my mother and I set out at long last to join my father in Germany. We drove to Tilbury Docks, where we met hundreds of other

1

families on their way to join menfolk on the Continent, and once again I have vivid memories of the journey.

By now I had reached the ripe age of six, and was not only able to understand what was going on, but also to appreciate more clearly the great significance of the voyage. I recall that everything seemed to take hours. I sat on top of our pile of luggage whilst my mother bustled about, coping with the might of military formalities. Children were everywhere, and occasionally a kindly WVS lady would pass by, dispensing tea or returning a lost infant to its parent. In the evening came the time to board the ship, an ex-German vessel now renamed the *Empire Halladale*. She was painted grey and buff, with splotches of rust everywhere, and was quite the biggest thing I had ever seen.

The delay ashore was followed by an equally lengthy process of cabin allocation and endless rehearsals of boat-drill. Everyone had to rush to their appointed lifeboat station wearing those heavy cork life-jackets, which in my case reached well down below my knees. The war had been over for a year and a half, but minefields still remained unswept, and the chance of hitting a drifting mine, I suppose, continued to be very possible. I remember the ship rolled heavily, making life on board very difficult, especially when it came to mealtimes. The children's nursery was on the upper deck, close to the lifeboats, and boat-drill continued to be practised twice a day. I recall the cramped cabin which we shared with another officer's wife and her daughter, and, last but not least, I well remember my poor mother being endlessly seasick.

The crossing lasted two and a half days, a journey which nowadays takes less than half that time, and on the morning of the third day, we docked at Cuxhaven, at the mouth of the river Elbe.

Excitement filled the ship, and I recall having my first glimpse of Germany through the cabin porthole that had leaked sea water all the way from the Thames estuary.

On the quayside, warrant-officers with white armbands rushed about in preparation for disembarkation. True to form, this was also slow to happen. A combination of the pouring rain and the late arrival of trains meant that families were held on board some hours after the ship's arrival, but eventually those for Hannover were called forward. At the bottom of the gangway each person was given an attractive little Union Jack brooch which had to be worn at all times to identify us, and which was, I suppose, the forerunner of the I.D. card.

The first official stop (there were many unofficial ones!) was at Hamburg, where families disembarking were soon completely

The author's father, Colonel Maurice Hurndall, near Bad Harzburg in the winter of 1945–46

soaked, for the roof of the Hauptbahnhof still lay in disrepair. For those remaining on board, tea and a packed meal were provided, and the journey continued. The train passed through villages where the local community lined the railway track, hopefully awaiting the odd apple or half-finished food parcel. Even at my age, it was disturbing to see people running like rabbits to retrieve others' left-overs. Long after dark, the train pulled into Hannover, and my father was standing on the platform. It was wonderful to be together again, and we had lots to talk about for the 30-mile drive to Hildesheim, where our first home was at Number 7 Haydnstrasse.

We lived in Germany for 13 years, with my father serving in seven different regional administrations during that time. My first formal schooling was at the Landschulheim, a private school on the outskirts of Holzminden on the river Weser. At the age of eight, I began attending boarding-school in England, crossing backwards and forwards from Harwich to the Hook of Holland for every holiday, aboard such grand old troopers as the *Empire Parkeston*, the *Vienna* and, quite the most uncomfortable ship ever built, the *Empire Wansbek*.

Our first years in Germany were not easy for my parents. Professionally, my father found much of the task very frustrating

3

with the enormous amount of red tape that hampered his work, whilst domestically, the absence of most simple household tools made home life a real challenge for my mother. Early in 1947, my father was appointed British Resident Officer in the university town of Göttingen in the south of the British Zone. In addition to the principal task of denazification, his responsibilities included the administration of the huge refugee camp at Friedland, close to the border with the Russian Zone, where all German POWs and displaced persons had to attend for re-registration. I often accompanied him on his many visits to the camp, and whilst attending his official functions, I used to wander around the compounds talking to some of the hundreds of homeless, destitute inmates, mostly as thin as their ribcages would allow, and all recently returned from POW camps in Russia or Poland. Elsewhere in Germany, evidence of the war remained well into the fifties, with burnt-out tanks, huge bomb craters and flattened cities for all the world to see.

Also not far from Friedland there was a large state orphanage, which my parents worked hard to improve. I loved to go with them on these visits and meet the children, especially at Christmas time. At the orphanage Christmas party in 1947, they gave me a small lotto game, beautifully handmade, which remains one of my greatest treasures to this day.

The author, aged seven, at the Friedland orphanage

4

It was during our first few days in Göttingen that we came upon a trunk full of Nazi Party journals, textbooks on the life of Adolf Hitler and the rise of the National Socialist German Workers Party (known as the NSDAP, or Nazi Party), along with hundreds of photographs, various items of uniform and regalia, and all hidden in the attic of our house, Number 60 Herzberger Landstrasse. Now, nearly 50 years later, with German reunification a reality and other dramatic changes in eastern Europe, it is a fitting time to translate these works into English, and remind ourselves of how an entire nation became swallowed up in hysterical fervour, according credence and support to a maniacal tyrant, Adolf Hitler. Events in the Middle East today lead the world to ask once again how it is that evil men come to wreak such havoc and destruction, resulting in so much sorrow and despair. The question will ever remain one of those tragic mysteries of history, and in the case of Adolf Hitler, has grieved thinking Germans for decades.

In fact, so great became this debate, that in 1953 a special committee of distinguished professionals was set up to try and establish fundamental reasons for Hitler's ability to seize power in Germany. They met at a Protestant seminary in a small town near Bonn, and were tasked with investigating, above all else, whether Hitler's rise to power was made possible by a unique set of circumstances, or whether it was a natural thing to expect in this land we know as Germany. The findings of the committee were never made public.

In compiling this book, I have therefore portrayed, on the one hand, the abhorrent rhetoric of Nazi propaganda texts as spoonfed direct to the German people, and on the other, a balancing account of 12 years' tyrannical rule by a despot whose blind fury and hysterical reasoning led directly to that nation's ruin. I trust the reader will find interest in differentiating one from the other and, in particular, find reward in the wealth of photographs, many of which have never been seen outside Germany.

To quote Winston Churchill, 'Many disasters, immeasurable cost and tribulation lay ahead, but there was no more doubt about the end.'

Christopher Hurndall
Bahrain, December 1994

Adolf Hitler, Nürnberg 1933

DEUTSCHLAND ERWACHT

Translation from an original text written by Heinrich Hoffmann, of the Nazi Party press office, as an introduction to the book *Deutschland Erwacht (Germany Reawakens)*, compiled for the Nazi Party propaganda department by SS Obersturmführer Felix Albrecht, Hamburg, 1933.

Fourteen years of struggle and strife has left precious little time to record events and compile a record of our brief yet valiant history. Much more important has been the never-ending task of conducting public gatherings, distributing party literature and preparing the daily tasks undertaken so courageously by our party leaders.

One of the earliest known photographs of Adolf Hitler, at a political rally in the Odeonsplatz, Munich, on August 1914

Adolf Hitler's unshakable belief that one day Germany would rise again has indeed come to glorious reality, and only now do we have the time to reflect on our brave heroes whose undying confidence and true loyalty has brought about this triumph against a world of such overwhelming enmity. Above all else,

7

we commemorate the founding members, whose victories and sacrifices have now earned them a place in the hearts of all.

Sadly, however, with the passage of time, many brave deeds have been forgotten, and, whilst others have not escaped recognition, it is important that each and every heroic deed be now brought to mind.

Founder members of the German Workers Party marching in Munich, 1921

Adolf Hitler and his gallant followers are today loved and admired by all the nation, and will be remembered evermore for their bitter struggle against hatred, enmity, slander and corruption. Even more than a remembrance to our fallen comrades, this work is dedicated to those national heroes whose brave deeds in the German Workers Party have so far remained concealed by the hostile press of the time. Only by carefully following the struggle of the past 14 years can one begin to understand Adolf Hitler, and truly recognise the magnitude of his leadership and conviction.

8

1

IN THE BEGINNING

The story of Hitler and his Nazi Party has its roots in the First World War. These hostilities had begun in the spirit of a punitive expedition of Austrian troops into Serbia, and lasted an unbelievable four and a half years. It involved human casualty and financial expenditure on such a vast scale that it brought down in ruins the three traditional empires of Austria, Russia and Germany.

A demonstration against ever worsening conditions, Munich Rathausplatz, 1923

Even the allies, victorious in battle, were left in total disillusionment at the end. Italy was near civil war, with a totally collapsed internal economy, whilst France, saddened and depressed by the enormous loss of life during the long years of fighting, had become very bitter and cynical. Great Britain, relatively powerful at the outbreak, had also suffered incredible losses, exacerbated by poor military leadership and serious differences between the Prime Minister and his commanders. Only the United States, which entered the war much later, emerged in 1918 relatively fresh and with its military might far from exhausted.

An early photograph of Hitler's *Sturmabteilung* (SA) or Storm Troopers, also known as the Brown-shirts

In order to conduct this war, Britain had either spent, or pledged, most of the great wealth in her overseas capital and credit. She had loaned vast sums to France and, in turn, had borrowed heavily from the United States. At the end, probably through sheer mental fatigue, the statesmen of the time were simply unable to comprehend the devastation in world economy that the war had brought. In 1918, Britain went to the polls with such slogans as 'Make Germany Pay', and 'Hang the Kaiser' as centre-pieces of Lloyd George's election campaign. The trouble was that such reparation could only be in the form of gold, and there was very little of that, or by the creation of exports, and there was none of that.

If things were bad in Britain, they were very much worse in Germany. Defeat had come suddenly. The Emperor, Kaiser Wilhelm II, had abdicated and fled to the Netherlands, and what was left of the nation was in political turmoil.

Storm Troopers on their way to a party rally, Munich, 1923

Two days before the signing of the Armistice, a group of German socialists led by Fritz Ebert declared themselves the new leaders of the German Republic. True, they were socialists and republicans, but they were not revolutionaries. They were men of courage and integrity who had tried to wrestle with a nation in collapse and establish a degree of lawful administration.

Germany's relationship with the Allies was regulated by the Treaty of Versailles, which declared the various lands that were to be handed over to the Allies, along with the new delineation of frontiers. Article 231, the famous 'Guilt Clause', stated that Germany alone must accept responsibility for the war. British feeling on the matter of 'responsibility' was mostly influenced by the 1914 German invasion of Belgium, a manoeuvre that Germans today like to gloss over. German thought, especially amongst those of higher moral standing, was that Germany was certainly responsible, but also that Austria and Russia should carry a share

11

of the blame. The newly formed administration, consisting mostly of socialists, centre leftists and democrats, accepted the treaty, including its war guilt clause, thus rendering itself from the outset utterly obnoxious to the majority of Germans.

Storm Troopers on the march in 1922, in the early days of the Workers Party movement. Note the motley collection of uniforms

The new constitution, instituted for the administration of the new Germany, was established in the small town of Weimar, in the province of Thüringen, until recently part of the German Democratic Republic. This relatively quiet location was intentionally chosen in order to remove the inevitable squabble from the already overheated atmosphere of the big cities. It was a constitution based on an extreme form of proportional representation, intended to be completely fair to every form of political opinion. In fact, it achieved the opposite, encouraging instead the growth of many small local parties, often with very radical views, and permitting them to attain heights of grossly exaggerated importance.

A notable feature of the war had been the rapid expansion of the German army, bringing with it a heavy demand for additional

Adolf Hitler studies the day's campaign route

Hitler (extreme right) calls a stop to read the papers

13

Despite arrest, he can still manage a '*Heil Hitler*'

officers. The regular officer corps had not been able to meet anything like the new demand, with the result that many men were commissioned into the officer ranks with neither the professional training nor the family background to equip them for the post. Most were young, in their mid-twenties, and faced unemployment when the war ended. They banded themselves together under the leadership of the highly decorated General Franz von Epp, who formed the quasi-military, and totally illegal, organisation known as the von Epp *Freikorps*. Nicknamed the *Kapp Putsch* and resembling some sort of buccaneering private legion, it soon became noted for its brutality and murderous activities especially

Adolf Hitler (centre) attending the National Day celebrations, Nürnberg, 1923

during its calamitous attempt to overthrow the authorities in Berlin.

Among von Epp's paid informers was his aide-de-camp, Captain Ernst Röhm, and a certain Lance-Corporal Adolf Hitler. Together they provided the necessary intelligence information, and raised the necessary funds, for the organisation's various subversive activities.

Hitler himself was now 30 years old. Born in the small Austrian

15

Adolf Hitler's birthplace, Guesthouse Josef Pommer

village of Braunau on the Inn, he was the illegitimate son of a 52-year-old Austrian customs officer, Alois Schickelgruber, and a young Czech-born peasant girl, Klara Poelzl. He had been a resentful, discontented child, of very unstable temperament and deeply hostile towards his strict, authoritarian father. In contrast, he became strongly attached to his hard-working mother, who dealt the adolescent young man a shattering blow when she suddenly died of cancer in December 1908.

His early choice of career was the arts. Fancying himself as a painter, at the age of 18 he left home for Vienna, where he hoped

Adolf Hitler, aged 33

17

to study at the Austrian Academy of Fine Art. His bohemian lifestyle, accompanied by his ever deepening hatred of Jews, Marxists, Liberalism and the Austrian monarchy, meant that he was rejected by the academy and left to earn a pittance hawking his sketches around the lesser-known taverns of the city. During his lonely and miserable years in Vienna, his frustration was part compensated for by his interest in conducting lively political speeches in cafés or on street corners – wherever he could find people willing to listen to him. He had never felt much respect for his own country, attaching himself instead to its Aryan neighbour, and the texts of his public harangues took on more and more the notion of a reawakened and glorious Germany.

It was also whilst in Vienna that he acquired his first education in politics, mostly from crackpot radical theorists and others equally obsessed with anti-Semitic feeling. He saw nothing in the Jewish ideology but chaos and corruption, and a determined conspiracy to exploit and undermine the purity of the German race.

His deep regard for Germany, together with his ambitious plans for the future, led him to move from Vienna to the Bavarian capital of Munich in the summer of 1913. Soon afterwards, he enlisted in the ranks of the 16th Bavarian Infantry Regiment and served as a battalion runner proving to be an able and courageous soldier. Eventually he was rewarded by promotion to the rank of lance-corporal, and reportedly received the Iron Cross for bravery. However, as this decoration was rarely, if ever, given to junior ranks, the award can be said to remain wrapped in a degree of questionable certainty. Twice wounded, and badly gassed only weeks before the war's end, he spent some months recuperating in a military hospital in Pomerania, now part of Poland. He was driven to blind rage by the news of Germany's defeat, and became convinced that fate had chosen him alone to rescue this humiliated nation from the shackles of the Versailles Treaty, from Bolsheviks and from Jews.

Meanwhile, the humble beginnings of the Nazi Party can be traced to a small drinking circle cum secret society, centred on one Anton Drexler, as early as March 1918. Joining forces with the political journalist Karl Harrer, and his comrade in arms Hermann Esser, Drexler founded the *Deutsche Arbeiter Partei*, the German Workers Party. Adolf Hitler, dispatched by von Epp to spy on this suspect organisation, decided by the end of that year to join its ranks himself, and imposed himself as chairman by the end of the summer of 1921. He introduced the swastika as the party's new symbol and the formal greeting '*Heil*' between members, and

General Franz von Epp, founder of the von Epp *Freikorps*

19

changed its name to the *Nationalsozialistische Deutsche Arbeiter Partei*, the National Socialist German Workers Party or Nazi Party.

By the end of 1921, Hitler was recognised as leader of a political faction numbering some 3,000 members, including his Storm Troopers (SA), set up to keep order at his meetings and break up those of his opponents. Under the leadership of his close associate Heinrich Himmler, Hitler formed his own personal bodyguard, the black-shirted *Schutzstaffel* (SS), which grew into the most powerful organisation within the Nazi Party.

He focused his propaganda against the Versailles Treaty, the Marxists and internal enemy number one, the Jews, whom he saw as responsible for Germany's monetary plight.

ADOLF HITLER

A personal tribute by SS Brigadier Julius Schreck, one of Hitler's closest and most loyal subjects, who assisted in the foundation of the SS Death's Head formations. Employed as specialist concentration camp guards, they were the toughest and most ruthless of all Nazi elements.

SS Brigadier Julius Schreck

21

What person is better known in the world today? On all continents and in all countries, the name Adolf Hitler has become the very symbol of hope and unity that millions of people, not only in Germany, have turned to with love and admiration, forcing his hitherto bitter opponents with much reluctance to accept his overwhelming qualities of leadership.

Apart perhaps from his date and place of birth, 20 April 1889 in the border village of Braunau on the Inn, what does the world really know of this unique man? Perhaps that he had had a difficult childhood, full of loneliness and hardship, that he enlisted as a volunteer soldier, was decorated in 1916, and that in ten laborious years he built up the National Socialist German Workers Party to be the most powerful political movement in the country.

Adolf Hitler

Yet this is still a small and incomplete picture. Only those whose education truly encompasses the life story of the Führer can really understand the destiny of this remarkable man. Today the people of Braunau am Inn proudly recall old Alois Hitler [real name Schickelgruber] the Austrian customs official and his beautiful wife Klara, whose third son we all know as Adolf.

The three boys grew up under the devoted care of their mother until, when Adolf was only five, the family moved to the larger town of Passau, then a year later, when his father retired, to the little Alpine village of Lambach. In 1897, he began attending the village school and, found to possess a beautiful singing voice, he joined the Sängerknaben, the boys' choir, in the local Benedictine monastery. It was here, whilst walking the cloisters of the monastery, that he first dreamed of that mystic emblem, the swastika, that would later become recognised the world over as the symbol of absolute power and supremacy.

In 1900, he moved to the grammar school in the city of Linz, where his father directed that he should study in order to become a government official too. Adolf had different ideas, and an irreconcilable argument developed when the 12-year-old

22

announced that he would become an artist.

He largely avoided school subjects in which he found little interest, although he thoroughly enjoyed lessons in geography and history in which he began to understand the true meaning of being a German and, equally important, of being a nationalist. Proudly wearing his red, white and black cocade and displaying all the youthful zeal of his age, he would greet people in the streets in the old German manner of 'Heil', and be heard to sing the national anthem, Deutschland, Deutschland über alles, even if it was pouring hailstones. This son of a customs officer was fast becoming a true German revolutionary.

The sudden death of his father in 1907 brought an end to the family squabbles, and Adolf Hitler enrolled at the Viennese College of Fine Art, but more tragedy was to befall him, for within a few months his beloved mother also passed away, leaving him now penniless and alone. At college he was told that rather than becoming an artist, he should study architecture, which would need diligent hard work, a discipline he had not considered whilst dreaming of becoming an artist.

He was now a member of the plebeian working classes, having to mix cement, carry stones and undertake strenuous labour in order to earn a living. During this difficult time, he learned the true meaning of Marxism, and saw how this poison was eating away at the very soul of the working man, at the same time realising that this doctrine was being perpetuated by the employers themselves, the Jewish business community. Hitler vowed to rescue the nation from this dilemma, and create a true socialism, incorporating not only the working classes, but all classes of German society.

If Adolf Hitler became a nationalist at school, he became a socialist whilst in Vienna. In 1912, with his restless mind now brimming with ideas of national socialism, he moved to the German city of Munich. He spent two happy years in this proud and art-filled state capital, until in 1914 the nation was brought headlong into conflict in the First World War. The Young Austrian didn't think twice. As an enthusiastic volunteer, he was appointed to the 16th Light Infantry Regiment, wherein he spent the next few years at the front. Assigned to the duty of dispatch-rider, he crossed the jaws of hell on countless occasions, successfully bringing vital messages through the lines. During the war years, he changed from being the impassioned volunteer to being a conscientious front-line soldier with an uncompromising desire to serve the Fatherland. In 1916 he was

The first banners of the Nazi Party

Adolf Hitler in the front-line trenches in the First World War

The only known photograph of General von Epp's *Freikorps* at a march past, Munich, 1919

wounded by shrapnel, but he soon returned to front-line service and was accorded the Iron Cross, First Class, for gallantry. [Once again, this award remains open to question.]

In Germany's battle to survive, Hitler not only learned the value of being a German soldier, but also the immense value of the German people and their nation, so that in later years when his path became so tortuous, he found much strength in the memories of his comrades and the soldiers of the war years.

In 1918, his regiment was again sent to the front, this time to the battlefield of Flanders, but whilst there, the German munitions workers went on strike, virtually crippling any last-minute attempt at saving the nation. The shadow of this revolt struck at the very heart of Germany's front-line soldier, and Hitler never forgave the social democrats for their barbarous act of treason.

In October of that year, with the war nearly at an end, Adolf Hitler was again wounded, this time by mustard gas from English artillery bombardment. Many were injured from these poisonous clouds, and with lung damage and half blind himself, he was brought to the von Beelitz military hospital in Pomerania, only to be told a short time later that Germany had surrendered.

Adolf Hitler (back row, second from right), shortly before release from hospital

Hitler found this news utterly repugnant, and whilst his eyesight was slowly recovering, he vowed to become a politician and strive to wash away the utter humiliation that had befallen the nation.

In March 1919, he returned to Munich and was appointed to serve on a regimental board of enquiry investigating the various consequences of the Russian Revolution. He began this new appointment as an education officer, assisting as an intelligence officer and political speaker. He became aware of the embryo German Workers Party, a small circle of barely half a dozen members, and despite its diminutive size, he realised that within this movement there could well lie the opportunities he was seeking and decided to join its ranks.

Good news

His membership number was seven, and under his direction the party was soon transformed into the National Socialist German Workers Party (NSDAP). In the grand banqueting hall of the Munich Hofbrauhaus, barely a year later, he announced the party's formal initiation, and his 25-point plan in which he spelt out the movement's future programme. Fourteen years of struggle and strife now lay before him.

On 9 November 1923, the new party's first rebellious outburst collapsed in the face of heavy rifle fire from the Bavarian state police. Hitler was taken prisoner to the fortress at Landsberg, and later charged with high treason.

The alliance seemed to have been crushed, but whilst imprisoned at Landsberg, he took the opportunity to publish his great work, Mein Kampf [My Struggle], *in which he unveiled the story of his life and his political ideology.*

He was released from prison on 20 December 1924, and on the very next day, he began working to revive the NSDAP. This time, he carefully chose a path of legality and integrity, announcing as he did so that he would beat them with their own weapons, declaring one evening in Munich's Bürgerkeller that once again the party was alive and well. Though hard and bloody the conflict, the new picture portrayed by the party, together with its leaders and its heroes, was soon apparent to the entire nation.

And so it was that Lance-Corporal Adolf Hitler became Chancellor of the German Empire. As a person, however, he never changed from what he always was, a kind, great yet gentle man, full of love for his country and its people without one hair of disloyalty.

An architect he indeed became, but an architect of a state, a nation and an empire. The first ever labourer to become an architect of a race of people.

2

MEIN KAMPF

Within two years of ending the First World War, the allies, and France in particular, were trying to squeeze reparations out of Germany, and not finding the task at all easy. Doubtless, some difficulties arose by reason of German procrastination, but in all fairness, the level had been set so high that effectual reparation was economically impossible.

By 1923, the French government had become so tired of the endless delays that they considered a military occupation of the industrial Ruhr district more than amply justified. On the other hand, the British government did not agree with such action, and consequently did not send troops to take part. For their part, the Germans resorted to the only means of defence at their disposal, namely passive resistance in the form of well-organised industrial strikes.

Hitler with Nazi leaders, Weimar, 1926

Before the French intervention, the German currency had already begun a downward slide, but with their policy of industrial action in the Ruhr proving so expensive, a final blow was dealt to the already overinflated Deutschmark. Inflation became rampant; in fact, prices rose so rapidly that soon barrel-loads of well-nigh worthless paper were needed to pay the wages of the smallest factory. Families with a lifetime record of prudent saving saw their wealth vanish overnight, and as the currency ceased to have any real value

29

Hermann Göring, Hitler's designated successor

at all, the proud professional and middle classes were soon reduced to the living standard of the ordinary working man. The complete disappearance of a nation's currency value struck a blow more widespread than any other calamity, and was to have a disastrous effect in the years to come.

Adolf Hitler, by this time joined in his convictions by the much respected if somewhat eccentric General Erich Ludendorff, had founded a nucleus of party leadership. It consisted of the aristocratic war hero and last commander of Baron von Richthofen's fighter squadron, Herman Göring; his close friend and fellow student of political science at the University of Munich, Rudolf Hess; and last but not least, the ruddy-faced swashbuckler, and his erstwhile mentor, Captain Ernst Röhm. Yet another prominent ideologist who played a leading role in shaping Hitler's ideas of both extreme nationalism and the eradication of Jews from society was one of the founder members of the German Workers Party, Gottfried Feder. Hitler regarded him very much as

German Day parade, Nürnberg, 1923, which set the form for similar parades over the next 22 years

a guide in economic and social affairs, although in the closing stages of the Third Reich, Feder's radical views and over-aggressive policies finally resulted in his dismissal from party affairs. In the earlier years, however, it was Feder's belief in complete Aryan racial supremacy that inspired Hitler to deliver the powerful and dramatic speeches which so dominated his audiences throughout his political life.

31

Marxists being driven away by Hitler's Storm Troopers

The National Socialists had been in existence for barely two years when, in the wake of such financial disorder, Hitler became convinced that the Weimar Republic was on the verge of collapse, and that the time had come to take action. Furthermore, persuaded by Röhm that the local army garrison would not offer any resistance, Adolf Hitler and his gang of disgruntled ex-soldiers seized upon the idea of overthrowing the state government of Bavaria. Motivated by the hatred and mistrust that Bavaria now felt for the Prussians and the Weimar agreement, he chose the fateful day of 9 November 1923 to burst into a popular Munich public house, the Bürgerkeller. Firing his pistol at the ceiling, he announced that he was about to head a new provisional state government which would immediately carry through a revolution against what he called 'Red Berlin'. Joined at his side by Ludendorff, Hess and Göring, he led a procession of some 3,000 men through the city's streets as far as the state parliament building, the Feldherrnhalle.

For their part, the Bavarian government had decided that the time had come to put an end to the bullying and subversive tactics of this relatively insignificant organisation, and met the marchers with a force of state police. The result was 16 dead, and many more injured. For Hitler, the day had been a catastrophe, and an ignominious end to the attempted overthrow. He himself fell to the ground early on in the brawl and, with a dislocated shoulder, was carried off in an ambulance. Managing to escape his police escort, he fled to the country home of another close friend, Ernst Hanfstängel, at Uffing in Bavaria but was recaptured two days later. As an Austrian citizen, he should have been extradited as an unwanted criminal there and then, but instead, following a dramatic court case in which he succeeded in turning the tables on his

Storm Troopers arriving to keep the peace at a rally in Oberwiesenfeld, Bavaria, 1 May 1923

accusers with a confident propagandist speech, he was sentenced to five years in prison. Had he indeed been returned to his native country, how different might have been the course of history.

Hess was similarly arrested and imprisoned, whilst Röhm was simply dismissed from military service, after which he fled to Bolivia and became an instructor in the Bolivian armed forces until he was recalled by Hitler two years later. Hermann Göring somehow escaped capture but, seriously wounded by gunshot, he too fled the country to Sweden, where he finished up in a mental hospital, becoming a complete morphine addict in the course of his slow recovery. The popular General Ludendorff, quite a national figure following his many victories in the Great War, knew that the police would not fire on him. Whilst others fell to

33

the ground in the volley of rifle fire, he calmly continued marching in between the muzzles, and, although arrested, he was subsequently acquitted at his trial. He remained a guardian of party affairs during Hitler's imprisonment, and stood as his candidate for the presidential election in 1925, but managed to gain little more than 1 per cent of the votes. This pronounced failure started a cooling-off in the relations between the two men, culminating ten years later in Ludendorff warning President Hindenburg that this sinister individual, Adolf Hitler, would one day lead Germany into the abyss of unprecedented disaster.

Ludendorff is, however, perhaps best remembered as the founder of a new German religious order called the Community of Believers, recognising and worshipping the ancient pagan Nordic gods. The doctrine was officially accepted by the Nazi Party in 1939, and not finally banned by the German government until May 1961.

Hitler was released after only nine months of his five-year sentence in Landsberg gaol, but during this time, he dictated his work *Mein Kampf* (*My Struggle*) to his staunch comrade and fellow prisoner, Rudolf Hess. The book, a very crude, ill-worded volume of primitive ideas, racial myth and strong anti-Semitic fervour, became the Bible of the Nazi Party, and by the start of the Second World War had sold over five million copies in 11 different languages.

Hitler's troops during the coup attempt of 9 November 1923

THE FOUNDATION OF THE NAZI PARTY

From a series of works by Heinrich Hoffmann of the Nazi Party press office

[Hoffmann first met Adolf Hitler whilst serving as a war correspondent during the First World War. They became very close friends, and through Hoffmann, Hitler met the two women in his life, Eva Braun, who worked in Hoffmann's photographer's shop, and Frau Winifred Wagner, the English-born wife of Siegfried Wagner, son of the famous composer. Hoffmann was appointed court photographer to Adolf Hitler, and was the only man permitted to photograph the Führer.]

The Führer on the Rhine, accompanied by his private photographer, Heinrich Hoffmann (right)

When, in the summer of 1919, the young intelligence officer Adolf Hitler was dispatched to report on a meeting of the German Workers Party, he little knew how important both for himself, and the entire world, the evening would be. In a small back room of the Sterneckerbräu public house in the centre of Munich, he found some 25 people attending a lecture on

The party's first offices, at the Sterneckerbräu tavern in Munich

political economics. Politically motivated perhaps, but certainly not a political movement, those present consisted of little more than a discussion group, listening to various addresses and debating the problems and worries of the time. When he came to leave, Adolf Hitler was presented with a small brochure entitled My Political Awakening *and written by one of the founders of the German Workers Party, the young labourer Anton Drexler.*

In this booklet, Adolf Hitler was reminded of the anguish and frustration he had suffered whilst living in Vienna as a young man, and when invited to a further meeting, this time as a guest, he was in no doubt about whether or not to attend. The gathering was held in the rather obscure location of the Alte Rosenbad tavern on the city's outskirts, and this time he was introduced to all six founder members. He found their visions of rescuing the country from the ever expanding ideals of Marxism and Communism not only very noble, but also very much in sympathy with his own, and following two days of thoughtful deliberation, decided to join himself, becoming the proud recipient of membership card number seven.

The group remained virtually unknown, however, and although their weekly meetings continued in the Café Gasteig, with busy discussions on correspondence received and current events, being only seven members meant that it was always the same seven at every venue, always in secret and rarely ending in any sort of mutual agreement. Hitler saw that if this alliance was to have any real meaning, then it had to be brought out of its shell, considerably enlarged and soundly financed. He set about the task of achieving this with no further delay, and began by distributing invitations for the next meeting, 80 in all, and each one hand-written. Still only 7 turned up, so he acquired an old typewriter, typed over 100 invitations for the next assembly, and this time 11 came. Then the numbers began to increase, 13, 17, 23, and within a month the crowd had risen to over 40. At this

latest meeting, a fund-raising made it possible to announce the following meeting in the daily press. The success was overwhelming, with 111 people turning up.

Hitler discovered a talent for delivering speeches and captivating audiences, especially as the numbers grew. He appealed to everyone's sense of pride and purpose, and at the next gathering, managed to swell the party's funds to a record 300 Deutschmarks, a fortune by anybody's standard. Furthermore, many younger people had been so fired up by the meeting and its speakers that they volunteered for more intensive duty at future assemblies.

The historic corner in the Café Gasteig where the original members of the Workers Party always met

The inscription on the wall reads (in translation): 'On 24 February 1920, our Chancellor, Adolf Hitler, founded the NSDAP in this corner. The foundations of the German freedom movement were laid here by the first seven valiant fighters'

37

As the year wore on, and the size of the gatherings grew, the evenings were not without some bloodshed. Hitler neither encouraged confrontation, nor did he avoid it, and as the size of his audiences continued to grow, Marxists and Communists tried in vain to prevent the meetings. In 1920, Adolf Hitler took over the chairmanship of the movement, introducing his famous 25-point plan, and changing the party's title from the German Workers Party, to the National Socialist German Workers Party, the NSDAP. No longer was Hitler working in obscurity. The Marxist press, realising that they had new enemies to contend with, began a programme of slanderous and vicious attacks, and then came a headlong clash between Adolf Hitler and his party colleage Harrer, who was convinced that Hitler was moving too fast.

A major assembly was arranged, this time in the very popular Hofbräuhaus in the centre of Munich, and in preparation, Hitler had excelled himself with leaflets, banners, flags and huge red posters to catch the eye. This upset the Marxists, who considered the colour red to be their own, but against an unexpected crowd of 2,000 cheering NSDAP followers, there was little they could do.

This first ever mass meeting was supposed to start at 7 p.m., with Adolf Hitler speaking at a quarter past. Worrying that he might not have enough people, he arrived in fact to face an overcrowded hall, but, as he soon realised, a hall half full of Communists, the people he really wanted to talk to. Within a few minutes, there was jostling, and Communists began fighting Hitler's supporters in the middle of the room. Hitler had taken the precaution of organising a strong-arm team of ex-army colleagues, who quickly cleared the chamber of all undesirables. Peace was restored, and once again his warm clear voice filled the hearts and minds of his attentive audience.

'The leaders of the party,' he cried out, 'swear to uphold the constitution of our 25-point plan, even if it means disregarding the safety of their own lives.' The assembly rose in a great cheering and clapping, and soon the meeting had won additional valuable friends like Fritz Pöhner, the state police chief, and Oberamtmann Wilhelm Frick, head of the police political wing and well known for his stand against Berlin.

Ten years later, Frick became Interior Minister in Hitler's government, but for the time being, the Bavarian state government had decided to ban the red placards as the ensuing crowds created a serious disturbance, although they didn't

Reich Minister Wilhelm Frick, head of the political police section of the Munich constabulary, and Hitler's close adviser and liaison man at police headquarters. He also took part in the 9 November 1923 putsch, and was also arrested, receiving a sentence of 15 months' imprisonment for his participation. He eventually rose to be Interior Minister in Hitler's government, and remained a loyal Nazi member all his life

object to the Marxists and Communists carrying them, as in their case the problem of security didn't exist. Because of this apparent discrimination, Hitler realised that he could not rely on government support, but he knew that he could rely on police assistance.

In December 1920, Hitler launched the party newspaper, the Völkischer Beobachter [Public Observer], *but continued to hold weekly meetings at the Hofbräuhaus, firmly believing a speech to be infinitely more powerful than a script.*

THE NATIONAL SOCIALIST GERMAN WORKERS PARTY, TWENTY-FIVE POINT PLAN

1. We demand the universal accord of all German people on the basis of the right to self-determination for a Gross Deutschland (*Greater Germany*).

2. We demand an equal right for Germany with regard to other neighbouring countries, and with it, the total annulment of the Versailles Treaty and the St Germain Agreement.

3. We demand land for our people, with the right to colonise in order to provide settlement for the population surplus.

4. We demand that only a person of true German blood, regardless of denomination, can be a national comrade, and only a national comrade can be a German citizen. This demand, therefore, means no person of Jewish descent can be a German citizen.

5. We demand that non-citizens can only reside in Germany as guests, and would be subject to the regulations relating to the residence of foreigners.

6. We demand that only German citizens have the right to determine the laws and the leadership of the nation, and therefore everyone in public office, whether state or federal, must be a German citizen.

7. We demand that the nation's first priority is the welfare and employment of its citizens, with the right to expel foreigners if necessary in order to achieve this.

8. We demand that any further entry of non-citizens into Germany be stopped immediately, and furthermore, that all non-citizens that entered Germany after the 22 August 1914 be repatriated.

9. We demand equal rights and duties for all German citizens.

10. We demand that the prime responsibility of all citizens will be intellectual or physical occupation, such work being for the benefit of the general public and not for its detriment.

11. We demand, therefore, the abolition of financial payments to the unemployed or to malingering members of the public, and an easing of interest burdens.

12. *In view of the enormous sacrifices made by the nation during the war period, and the inevitable profits made by some, we demand that such profit-taking be deemed a criminal act, and all such wartime proceeds be confiscated.*

13. *We demand the nationalisation of all remaining unnationalised companies and trusts.*

14. *We demand the sharing out of profits from large companies and corporations.*

15. *We demand a sizeable increase in benefits for the aged.*

16. *We demand the creation of a healthy middle class and its social protection and, in conjunction, the transfer of private business complexes to local authorities for the purpose of leasing to small-time traders at low rentals, provided such traders' business is for the general well-being of the people or the state.*

17. *We demand that laws pertaining to land reform be brought in line with present-day necessity, and regulations be enacted permitting the derequisitioning of land and its transfer without charge for the benefit of the people. Ground-tax laws to be abolished, and any possibility of property speculation to be prevented.*

18. *We demand a ruthless crack-down on all those whose activities are seen to be harming the common interest. Criminals, profiteers and anyone involved in black-market dealing will receive the death sentence on conviction, without consideration of mitigation or racial origin.*

19. *We demand a replacement of the existing outdated and purely materialistic Roman law by a new German common law.*

20. *We demand the immediate reorganisation of the state education system, whereby all hard-working and intellectual Germans will have the opportunity of receiving tertiary education, and thereby attaining positions in higher management. The curriculum of all educational establishments must be geared to present-day practical requirements, and must include basic instruction in the ideology of National Socialism.*
    We further demand the education of specially talented children at public expense, without having regard to their

parents' occupation or social standing.

21. *We demand an immediate improvement to the state's programme of health care, in particular, better support of mother and child, prevention of under-age employment, establishment of state training centres for sport and greater assistance for organisations dedicated to the physical training of our youth.*

22. *We demand the establishment of a people's army and the total abolition of all mercenary forces.*

23. *We demand laws preventing the spreading of political untruths by the press and public media.*
   In order to provide a worthy German press, we demand that,
   i) *All editors and employees of newspapers published in the German language must be national comrades of Germany.*
   ii) *All non-German newspapers need express approval from the state before their distribution, and such newspapers may not be printed in the German language.*
   iii) *Legislation be enacted prohibiting non-Germans from financial benefit in the press, or in any way influencing the content of a German newspaper. Punishment for contravention of this law to be immediate deportation and closure of the newspaper concerned. Newspapers seen to contain offensive material or matters contrary to the public interest to be closed down. Similarly, production of any art form or literature undermining public life will be prohibited.*

24. *We demand complete freedom of religious practice in the state, providing that no such devotion endangers the moral feelings of the Germanic race. Fundamentally, the National Socialist German Workers Party, (NSDAP) supports the Christian faith, without binding itself to any particular persuasion. The party wholly condemns the Jewish materialistic spirit, and suggests that permanent recovery of this nation can only be effected on the basis of 'Public service before personal interest'.*

25. *In order to implement this programme of national reconstruction, we demand the creation of one central*

authority, having control and jurisdiction of all political activities throughout the Reich. Professional and occupational associations are to be formed at state level to implement the Reich's enacted laws, and to provide guidelines to individuals on matters of personal and corporate conduct. [The Rahmengesetze, as they were termed, meaning 'Laws of Framework'.]

Party leaders ruthlessly swear to uphold this 25-point plan, if necessary under sacrifice of their own lives.

The Communists, for their part, tried both ignoring the meetings and breaking them up, but neither tactic was of much consequence. In fact, many Communists crossed over to become members of the NSDAP.

To give Hitler's strong-arm squads some degree of recognition, he introduced a brown windcheater with red swastika armband. Consisting of ex-soldiers, labourers and students, and proudly wearing this new uniform, they gallantly met fear with fear and terror with more terror, and by 1921, over 100 groups of such strong-arm combatants were in existence, out of which he formed the SA or Sturmabteilung.

An idea, a community, a state, even a nation, needs a symbol to lighten the hearts of the people and provide a focal point for their pride and devotion. The Marxists had their banners and red cockades, and now Hitler presented the party with his symbol, the black swastika on the red flag, a symbol of sweeping change and wondrous beauty, to be followed two years later by the party standard of a flying eagle with wreathed swastika in its talons.

Following the first mass gathering in the Munich Hofbräuhaus, the movement quickly gathered momentum, until by the end of 1921 the number of registered members exceeded 6,000. By now, Hitler was in sole command of the NSDAP, and with its reputation improving daily, it was only a matter of time before a major clash with the Communists took place. With the date set on 4 November, when Hitler had planned another mass meeting, the Communists decided to blow up the Hofbräuhaus, together with everyone inside. One hour before events were due to start, Hitler was advised of the Reds' dastardly plan and personally addressed every Storm Trooper present, urging them to give of their very best should the usual trouble break out. Unfortunately, the party's administrators had also chosen that day to move its headquarters to another location, Number 10 Corneliusstrasse, as the previous offices had become too small. This operation left only 46 troops to guard the meeting, and although the Communists abandoned their idea of blowing the place up, when the signal was given, there wasn't a man seen not bleeding profusely. The Communists attacked with beer mugs and broken bottles, but after 30 minutes the gallant Storm Troopers gained the upper hand, chasing them out of the building and shooting at them as they fled down the street.

It was at this gathering that Adolf Hitler bestowed the title 'Sturmabteiling' on his devoted men. From then on, the

Number 10 Corneliusstrasse, the party's second headquarters

movement marched from one meeting to another, protected by the proud SA, who in turn chalked up one victory after another against the party's undesirable opponents. Windcheaters gave way to fully fledged brown uniforms, and the SA became known as the brown brigade.

There was now hardly a soul in Munich who had not heard of the NSDAP and its swastika emblem, for the movement had become a power to reckon with in the city. Hitler continued to make it clear that his SA men were a part of the party, albeit mobile in formation in their task of protection, but not in any way a military organisation. They had had to be re-educated, not in a martial sense, but in a political one, with discipline rather more voluntarily than militarily established. In his book Mein Kampf, *Hitler had written 'What we needed was not one or two hundred bold conspirators, but thousands of fanatical followers of the party's cause. We could not have won by the sword or pistol, but only by mass demonstrations and conquests of the streets, for it is the master of the street that will become master of the nation.'*

The SA's first parade and march past was staged in Munich in protest against new laws supposedly designed to protect the republican status of the nation. Several hundred marchers, many carrying the red flag with swastika emblem, soon ran into lines of Communist opponents, but as most of the crowd were by now chanting in support of the NSDAP, any possible confrontation was soon dispersed. The success of this first march became known all over Germany with the result that in October 1922, the Central Committee of National Associations invited Adolf Hitler and a few of his companions to attend the German Day celebrations being held that year in Coburg. Hitler decided that a few companions could be stretched to some 800 SA troopers, and he chartered a special train to take them all with him. Met at Coburg station by members of the committee, he was instructed that there was to be no marching in closed ranks, no carrying of party banners or flags, and no bands. Utterly outraged, he vehemently denounced such restrictions and promptly marched at the head of his contingent to the Hofbräuhaus Keller in the centre of the city, calmly ignoring the abuse and protests of the surrounding crowds.

NSDAP members attending the German Day rally in Coburg, October 1922

The police, equally calmly, lined the route to the city centre, only to lock up all the doors of the Hofbräuhaus as soon as the last SA guard entered the building. Hitler was by now raging with fury and, in threatening language, insisted his men be let out. With some reluctance, the police eventually succumbed, unlocking the doors and permitting the marchers to return to the station. The crowds had become equally indignant, and began throwing bottles and stones. The long-suffering SA squads, who equally well had had enough, broke ranks, and in ten minutes cleared the streets of all the competition. Minor scuffles continued throughout the night, but by the following morning, a warm, bright Sunday, any Communist terror in Coburg had been put to flight.

The success of the visit can be truly measured when, two years later, Coburg became the first German city to have a National Socialist majority, and the first city to produce a National Socialist Bürgermeister. [Mayor]

Returning to the station later in the day, Hitler found his train staff, having been threatened by Communists, refusing to operate the train. Within 15 minutes, however, he had completely restored their loyalty, and the trainload of triumphant SA guards departed on time.

In 1923, Hitler entrusted the leadership of his gallant SA to Hermann Göring, who soon went on to defeat further Communist threats in other Bavarian cities, eventually purging the entire nation of the Marxist and Communist menace, and reinstating the freedom of speech to every man in the street. Once again, Hitler was at pains to define how he wanted the SA to be. They were not to be seen as a military organisation or a secret militia, but instead they were to be well versed in National Socialist ideology, well practised in physical training, and above all else, superbly disciplined. As that year dawned, however, the development of this political task force was to change, with many of its heroes falling to the sword before the year was out.

France had occupied the profitable Ruhr district since the end of the First World War, and in September of that year, in a massive and bloody uprising, Germany's passive resistance to this occupation suddenly ended, with a worker, Leo Schlageter, becoming the first man to lose his life in the cause of National Socialism. Following the complete collapse of the party in November of that year, it was the physical discipline and political indoctrination of the SA that, above all else, led to the rekindling of the NSDAP two years later.

[The reference here is to Hitler's abortive march against the Bavarian state government, as covered in the previous chapter, and lightly glossed over in this presentation.]

48

Hermann Göring, upon appointment as leader of the SA in August 1923

Police barricades erected against the NSDAP march of 9 November 1923, in Munich

ADOLF HITLER'S TRIAL AND IMPRISONMENT

NSDAP press release following Hitler's release from Landsberg Prison, December 1924.

On a grey, windy day in February 1924, with a cordon thrown around the Munich Criminal Court, the police were struggling to hold back the crowds of people trying to enter. The occasion was the public trial of Adolf Hitler and his comrades, the charges, high treason, and other offences against the state. Inside, the courtroom was packed. There were state police in green uniforms, city police in blue uniforms, barricades across every doorway, and the tightest security the city had ever seen.

Eventually, clerks reported the assembly under control, and as Hitler and his accomplices entered the court, a hushed wave of sympathy and compassion filled the chamber.

Proudly displaying his Iron Cross, and flanked on one side by Frick and Pöhner, and on the other by Kriebel and General Ludendorff, Hitler stood in the dock to receive the Chief Justice's opening address. 'Herr Hitler,' he said, 'kindly describe to the court the pattern of your life so far.'

The question was exactly what Hitler wanted, and for the next four hours he delivered a most brilliant and resounding speech. Everyone in the courtroom smiled, even the walls seemed to smile, as he stood alone and tactfully turned the tables on his accusers, whilst outside hundreds more people listened to the proceedings through the loudspeakers. 'By God, this is not the voice of an accused,' everyone was saying, 'it is the voice of a relentless accuser,' as his words burnt, like flames, the hearts and minds of his audience.

In his speech, he talked about his life in Vienna, the frustration, the hunger, Marxism and the universal curse of Judaism. 'I left Vienna as an anti-Semite and ardent enemy of Marxism,' he said.

The words fell like thunder on the ears of everyone present as he proceeded to describe his role in the Great War and the subsequent civil revolt of 1918. He talked about the first seven years of National Socialism, the Sturmabteilung, running battles with Communists in the streets and public houses of Munich, even the visit to Coburg and the quelling of Communist-inspired riots by his men.

Despite the thunderous applause that filled the courtroom each time he paused, his speech had only just begun. Continuing with

The original party banner, carried at the 9 November putsch and subsequently paraded at most NSDAP gatherings

an attack on the politics and treachery of the Bavarian State Commissioner, Hermann von Kahr and his government, he described the unforgivable shooting at the Feldherrnhalle on 9 November. 'What was the government supposed to be doing,' Hitler challenged the court, to yet another tumultuous applause, 'and why had a division of state troops been held back in Munich for a secret operation known only to von Kahr?' With so many outbursts of tumultuous applause, the judge was often obliged to halt the proceedings whilst the crowd was brought under control. 'On the matter of the 9 November killings,' Hitler eventually announced, 'I personally gave the order for the demonstration, knowing perfectly well that von Kahr and his associates Loussow and Seissner were fully behind me, and equally well, wanted to see an end to the present appalling state of affairs in the nation. It would have been madness to carry out this act without assurance of state co-operation.'

[High treason carried the death sentence in Germany, and Hitler's line of defence, if it can be so termed, was to show first of all that the state government was supposed to have been behind him, and secondly, to uncover a plot by State Commissioner von Kahr to carry out a *coup d'état* himself immediately after Hitler's arrest, and in so doing, split Bavaria apart from the rest of Germany. In fact, Hitler had been advised by General Ludendorff, quite mistakenly, that the state police would not open fire on the demonstrators, and that the government would accept his 'decree of change', to have been presented on the steps of the Feldherrnhalle.]

'I am therefore most surprised,' Adolf Hitler went on, 'not to find von Kahr, Loussow and Colonel Seissner, who after all were planning real acts of treason, sitting here next to me.'

'You judges of the case,' he concluded, 'can condemn us, pronounce us guilty, but in time the goddess of truth and eternal history will smile on this day, tear up this judgement, and set us free from all blame and wrongdoing.'

The cheering was unbelievable. Never before had a man charged with high treason spoken out in such a magnificent way. Hitler was followed on the stand by Dr Weber, who also condemned the deceitful politics of von Kahr, further revealing plans to introduce a separate currency for Bavaria, which would have richly lined von Kahr's pockets in the process. He also testified that, only three days before the November putsch, von Kahr had given his full support to the plot, and that the Bavarian People's Party leader, Dr Heim, had been conducting secret negotiations with the French authorities on the question of the Ruhr and its partial transfer to Bavaria. Guilt and more guilt, but no longer on the shoulders of the accused.

Five days after the trial commenced, counsel for the defence began filing for the arrest of von Kahr, Loussow and Seissner on charges of murder and high treason. The case became a war of words, and when such an expression as 'November criminals' began to be heard in testimony, Adolf Hitler jumped to his feet shouting, 'November criminals, it was I that took charge of political action to crush the November criminals.'

'It is my right,' he continued, 'if not today, then at some future date, to show exactly who were the true November criminals.'

That day, the court saw history in the making. Von Kahr was called to testify, and following the case for the prosecution, Hitler's own attorney was on his feet, delivering a further barrage of embarrassing questions.

'Why did you hold back a division of troops in Munich? And why did you confiscate the state gold stock held in the Reichsbank in Nürnberg?'

'For what reason did you suddenly visit Thüringen immediately prior to the 9 November putsch? And finally he asked, 'Why did you tell the state publishers in Stuttgart, on the matter of publishing a new party manifesto, that you couldn't wait much longer?'

[All these questions seem somewhat disjointed and out of context nowadays, but at the time would have instilled much fear and embarrassment in the Bavarian state government.]

Von Kahr couldn't, or wouldn't answer these questions. He assured the court that he was not able to recall, and he never dared to present any sort of defence. The only statement that he did make was a very obvious fabrication, and when he left the courtroom, everybody stepped back, many turning their heads away in disgust.

As the trial continued, Hitler's position slowly changed from being defendent to that of prosecutor. Sufficient evidence had been presented to show that von Kahr had indeed intended to carry out a massive coup d'état, not simply a show of political expression as Hitler had intended, but a revolt of grave consequence which would have split Bavaria apart from the rest of Germany, and Hitler's attempt to prevent this, even to the extent of damaging his own cause, was by then far more than apparent.

The case came to an end on 30 March 1924, and on the

following day, sentence was to be pronounced. Every available policeman was drafted into the city, and crowds shouting 'Heil Hitler' walked alongside his defence counsel on their way to the court. Arrangements had been made for Hitler to leave the courthouse in an open car unless the death sentence was pronounced, in which case, the vehicle would doubtless be closed. Finally, what everyone had been waiting for, the judgement and pronouncement of punishment, Ludendorff set free, Frick and Brückner 18 months imprisonment, Weber, Kriebel and Hitler five years in maximum security but with a probationary clause that the sentence be reviewed after six months.

The crowds went wild, and for a man that had volunteered to spend more than four years at the front and who now considered himself to be a total German, their jubilation showed more than sufficient justification for his actions.

In dismay, von Kahr's supporters witnessed the emotions of a nation, whilst Adolf Hitler's followers continued their celebrations well into the night. Five years in a maximum security prison for a man who only wanted the best for his people! On 1 April, Hitler walked for the second time in his life through the gates of Landsberg fortress, this time not in protective custody, but as a convicted man. His room was very bare, just an iron bed, a mattress, blankets, one small table and two chairs. From the barred window, and beyond the high compound wall, he could see the fields and farmhouses of Landsberg village, and in this lovely, isolated world, the Führer settled down to create his greatest work, Mein Kampf [My Struggle].

[Incidentally, the writing paper upon which this book was first written was sent to Hitler by the English lady, Winifred Wagner, born Winifred Williams, widow of Siegfried Wagner, the son of the famous composer. In later years, her relationship with him became so intimate that there was even talk of marriage, and Haus Wahnfried, the Wagner family home, became one of Hitler's favourite retreats.]

On 20 April 1924 Hitler reached his 35th birthday. If the powers that be had thought that, tucked away in prison, he would soon be forgotten about, they couldn't have been more wrong. That day, the postman delivered more letters, telegrams and parcels to Landsberg fortress than was normally brought in a year, and Hitler's cell was a sea of flowers.

By the autumn, the number of inmates had grown to 32. There were days of happiness and others of despair. They all had

Hitler in his cell in Landsberg prison

*families and friends to occupy their minds, and in the evenings
the Führer would gather them together, read passages from his
new book, and fill their hearts with hope and confidence once
again.*

Day after day the Führer worked on his album, whilst his comrades spent their time working in the prison compound, clearing paths, chopping firewood or planting trees and shrubs, anything to while away the time.

At ten o'clock, on the evening of 19 December, with most of the prison staff and inmates in bed, the Director of Landsberg made a personal visit to Adolf Hitler's cell, and informed him that he was a free man. Very early next morning, everyone in the prison gathered together to bid farewell to the Führer, for by now even the staff had become National Socialists. Hitler shook hands with each and every man, and in handing over his position as senior inmate to his deputy, Rudolf Hess, he announced that he would do everything in his power to have everyone released as soon as possible.

Hitler on his release from Landsberg, having served only nine months of a five-year sentence

The Director was waiting for Hitler at the outer gateway, and as he also shook hands and bad him goodbye, he said proudly, 'I think I too am a National Socialist!'

The Führer returned immediately to head his National Socialist movement once again, announcing to the press that in five years he would rebuild the party to its previous strength.

He wasn't wrong.

Hitler, soon after his release from gaol, visits a farming community in East Prussia

Children celebrate Hitler's release from prison

The first announcement that the NSDAP was to be revived, following Hitler's release from Landsberg prison

Adolf Hitler pays a nostalgic visit to Landsberg ten years later

59

3

GERMANY DURING THE TIME OF HITLER'S IMPRISONMENT

Whilst Adolf Hitler remained in Landsberg gaol, the situation in Germany slowly began to improve. The Foreign Minister, Dr Stresemann of the *Deutsche Volkspartei* (the German People's Party), had decided to break off the costly struggle with France over the occupation of the Ruhr district, whilst for their part, the French government was equally glad to see an end to the complicated issue. The worthless paper money was replaced by the *Rentenmark*, the brainchild of one Hjalmar Schacht, who, some years later, served as the financial wizard of the Third Reich. On behalf of Germany, he negotiated the Dawes Plan, a complex programme of aid and reparation settlement not dissimilar to the Marshall Plan of 1947. This scheme paved the way for the first sensible and practical solution to Germany's economic dilemma.

The earliest followers of Adolf Hitler, in 1922

In 1924, a new treaty was signed by Chamberlain for Great Britain, Briand for France and Stresemann for Germany, providing for the withdrawal of French troops and heralding a new period of European co-operation.

The failure of the 'Beer Hall Putsch', as it was later called, and his subsequent imprisonment had transformed Hitler from a wild adventurer into a shrewd political tactician. He realised that the only way to power lay through apparent subversion of the existing constitution rather than through irresponsible acts of force, though he did conclude that a little street terror and intimidation would do no harm in establishing a mass movement and its political strength.

A year after the Munich fiasco, the first post-war President of Germany, Franz Ebert, died, and in his place the aged but much loved, Marshal Paul von Hindenburg was elected.

The Dawes Plan involved the injection of considerable funds from America, from which Germany paid reparations to the allies, who, in turn, repaid their debts to America. Unlike the Marshall Plan of later years, however, these funds were all from private sources, and this unexpected flow of gold into Germany soon allowed for the re-equipping of factories, the reconstruction of working-class housing and the return to international trade.

Göbbels visiting Adolf Hitler's home in the Obersalzberg

With Hindenburg as President, and with the able guidance of Stresemann and his colleagues, propaganda from Adolf Hitler could only hope for limited success. It was, however, during this period of relative calm that Hitler did manage to recruit one of his most able and cunning lieutenants, Dr Joseph Göbbels.

Göbbels suffered, above all else, from an acute inferiority complex which when coupled with his general contempt for the human race, made him a very desperate and dangerous man.

He had been well educated, but was refused entry into military service because of a crippled foot, the result of polio as a young child, and because of his very weak and diminutive frame. He had at first sought refuge behind a bohemian lifestyle as a poet/dramatist, but his literary efforts were all failures until, in 1927, he began editing his own weekly newspaper, *Der Angriff* (*The Attack*). He organised street battles and shooting affrays in back alleys, and soon became the most feared demagogue of the city of Berlin. At one stage, he even advocated the expulsion of the 'petty bourgeois' Adolf Hitler from the ranks of the NSDAP, but he soon switched to Hitler's side when offered the post of Party Reichs Propaganda Minister in May 1929. (If anyone can be accused of inducing the surrender of the German masses and feeding the people with the mythical image of a Messiah/Redeemer, it is indeed Joseph Göbbels.)

Hitler had cause to be grateful to this little man, for without him the management and manipulation of the masses would not have been so easy; whilst Göbbels himself at last found his mission in life, selling Hitler to the German people and orchestrating the pseudo-religious cult of the Führer as the saviour of Germany.

Hitler with Göbbel's daughter Helga

62

DR JOSEPH PAUL GÖBBELS

A personal tribute by Heinrich Hoffmann of the Nazi Party Press Office.

A brilliant socialist and never far from Hitler's side, Joseph Göbbels was born of Catholic working-class parents in the traditional Rhineland town of Rheydt and, like the Führer, possessed exceptional qualities of intelligence and leadership.

Despite the enormous struggles and prevarication of early years in the party, there was never one word of bitterness or personal insult heard against Göbbels in his home town, for here he was so well known that no amount of political agitation could undermine his popularity.

His youth was overshadowed by his experiences during the Great War, which, as he lived so close to the border, were particularly bitter. Whilst nearby the sound of shell fire could be heard day and night, at home the young student threw himself wholly into his studies, determined to give of his best for the good of the nation. His period of study saw the end of hostilities and the outbreak of civil revolution, which left the despondent young man with the feeling that all his effort had been in vain.

Restlessly, he moved from one university to another, finding little hope or purpose in life, until almost despairingly, he moved to the city of Munich in 1922. Here he was invited to attend a political meeting of the National Socialist German Workers Party, where he heard Adolf Hitler speaking, and for the first time in over four years, he felt a spark of hope kindling in his heart.

The Führer spoke for two hours, and as Göbbels listened, his own dreams of a new socialist Germany suddenly began to make sense. Hitler seemed to move mountains, and now Göbbels felt that to follow him would be no disgrace; in fact, on the contrary, it could be the turning-point in his life. Follow him he did, and for his first assignment he was dispatched, along with many others, to the Ruhr industrial district to set up an active political movement resisting not only the occupying powers, but to counter the very system that had allowed such occupation to take place. Here in the Ruhr struggle, Göbbels learned about the secret weapon of propaganda and the valuable part it played in clandestine operations. He was able to motivate the people around him and lead them side by side in community projects, whatever background, class or education

Joseph Paul Göbbels

they possessed. Labourers alongside soldiers, students alongside the bourgeoisie, industrialists and unemployed, all in the service of Germany. He also realised that by eliminating the Marxist press, Germany's poorest citizens soon became his most trusted companions.

Göbbels chats to a member of the Hitler Youth

He visited thousands of poor working families in their wretched little flats, he sat with miners deep underground, and he crept through streets and alleyways, night after night, organising frays and disturbances aimed at disrupting the puppet administration. He listened to labourers, students, farmers and soldiers, and all to determine how best to tackle the diseases of a decaying nation.

In November 1923, as traitors' bullets suddenly brought party affairs to an end and all forms of passive resistance had been outlawed, Göbbels summoned up more courage, and under threat from both the occupying forces and Germany's Bolshevik population, quietly continued his work of civil unrest and public disorder. During his later years in Berlin, when once again he lived under constant pressure, he would benefit enormously from the experiences he gained during these difficult years in the Ruhr.

65

The period 1923 to 1926 saw Göbbels achieving ever more success in his determined fight for the freedom of the National Socialist movement, with the eventual prize being the sight of Hitler's banners standing proudly where once only the red banners of the Communists were to be found. It was his outstanding success in the Ruhr that enabled hundreds of labourers to travel to Weimar in 1926 and take part in the Führer's first major party convention, a feat which Adolf Hitler never forgot and which led not only to a lasting friendship between the two men, but also to Göbbels' further reassignment to perhaps the hardest task Hitler had to face, Berlin! A city of some four million people, Berlin was the heartbeat of the Reich, and the daunting challenge now facing Dr Göbbels was to win this city for National Socialism and the swastika, against an overwhelming majority of social democrats and hard-line Communists.

Göbbels speaking at an election rally in Berlin

Despite Berlin being the seat of the Prussian government, with their strict policies of suppressing any attempt at national front formations, Göbbels never hesitated in his apparently hopeless task. Within a few months of taking up the appointment, he had succeeded in unifying all the various divided factions of National Socialism, and by dismissing unreliable or untrustworthy members, he bound together all those remaining into one single steel-minded and determined fighting unit. Under his leadership, the Berlin Sturmabteilung soon became a feared and powerful band of champions.

[It should be remembered here that during Göbbels' latter days in the Ruhr, he was co-author of the draft proposal submitted at the Hannover conference of 1926 that called for the expulsion of Adolf Hitler from the National Socialist Party. Once again, his shrewd political instinct was demonstrated by his sudden shift to Hitler's side later in the same year, when offered the post of Gauleiter of Berlin.]

Göbbels at his desk at the Ministry of Information and Propaganda, with his private secretary

Göbbels' successful reorganisation of the movement in Berlin was never better seen than in the alarming battle against the Communists in the Pharussäle district, hitherto established as

67

the main assembly place for gentlemen of the Soviet star. The brawl lasted barely 30 minutes, during which the Communists suffered many seriously injured and, in the end, experienced their first defeat, leaving Hitler's swastika flag flying victoriously over the rubble and ruin. Despite the ban on public gatherings and the terror in the streets, Joseph Göbbels managed within one year to send a detachment of 700 Sturmabteilung to the next party convention at Nürnberg. No matter how much the movement was outlawed, this fanatical fighter witnessed more and more people gather around the banner of Adolf Hitler and his belief in National Socialism. He also founded the party newspaper, Der Angriff (The Attack), thereby achieving what everybody thought to be madness, a powerful weapon in the struggle for Berlin.

By 1932, Göbbels was able to present the Führer with a city in which his flag was to be seen everywhere, and in which hundreds of thousands had declared their allegiance to the party. An élite troop of Sturmabteilung stood guard night and day in pursuit of their duty, quite prepared to defend to their death the honour and discipline that National Socialism demanded.

Sports areas and indoor tennis courts were often overcrowded, as more and more people gathered to listen to speeches by Dr Göbbels or, on rare occasions, the Führer himself. The city's streets, now free from Marxist terror, could be heard echoing to the marching of Hitler's brown-shirted revolutionaries, and the work of four years' unimaginable struggle by his foremost Fieldmarshal, the victorious Gauleiter and darling of Berlin, Joseph Göbbels. On the other hand, as the most hated enemy of the Marxists, Göbbels was perpetually and slanderously ridiculed by the Left, who bestowed on him the nickname 'Superbandit of Berlin'. This animosity, however, was more than matched by the admiration and popularity demonstrated by his followers, who affectionately called him 'The Doctor'. In 1929, in recognition of his outstanding service to the party, Hitler appointed him Reich Minister for Education and Propaganda.

As a propagandist, it was hardly necessary to describe Göbbels any further. His genius for writing, and his perseverance in campaigning, were qualities recognised the world over, and yet these attributes could never have had the success they did, had they not been based right from the start on absolute truth and integrity. Never for one moment did Göbbels try and fool the people; on the contrary, he always

68

Adolf Hitler, flanked by Stresemann and Göbbels, at a rally in Berlin

spoke bluntly and resolutely, preferring to leave tactics of fraud and deception to the social democrats and the 36 other political movements to be found within the city. His speeches were always centred on reality and conviction, encouraging constant readiness, courage and belief in the Führer. With one superb effort, he directed the people along the straight path towards one supreme goal, the man, Adolf Hitler, the ideal, the National Socialist German Workers Party. These two beliefs alone, he declared, would save Germany, and with it, every living German being.

Another participant in the Munich Beer Hall Putsch, albeit only as a standard-bearer, was Heinrich Himmler. As a young man, he had been in and out of the political scene, until in 1925 he became assistant head of the Nazi propaganda machine, rising four years later to lead Hitler's newly formed personal bodyguard, the *Schutzstaffel* (SS).

Heinrich Himmler (extreme right) accompanies Hitler to a rally of *Sturmabteilung* and *Schutzstaffel* divisions in 1929

Under his direction, this much-feared legion of black-shirted, hand-picked men grew from a small body of some 200 to something in excess of 52,000 by 1933. Within a further three years, he had successfully completed his bid to win control of the entire political and criminal police throughout Germany. As can be imagined, he was a meticulous administrator, with an astonishing capacity for work, which showed itself in his rapid accumulation of official appointments and in his efficient eradication of all opponents of the Nazi regime. In 1933 he instituted the first concentration camp at Dachau, near Munich, appointing Theodor Eicke as Commandant and introducing the skull and crossbow cap badge of the SS Death's Head units. Not only was this establishment soon followed by many more, but also by a far wider range of persons qualifying for internment. His fanatical obsession with racialism and commitment to Aryan supremacy was highlighted in his notorious speech to the German people in 1937, in which he announced his determination to exterminate all 'subhumans' the world over who are, in any way, opposed to Germany, the 'chosen custodian of human culture and world power'. Discipline and control within the camps was presided over by his Death's Head SS officers, whilst his romantic dream of blue-eyed, blond-haired heroes was to be achieved by the establishment of a state-registered human stud-farm, where young girls of perfect Nordic lineament would procreate with chosen SS men, and in which the offspring would be better cared for than in the very best maternity homes.

ADOLF HITLER, HIS SA AND HIS SS

From Germany Reawakens by Obersturmführer Felix Albrecht, 1933.

The interminable struggle of the NSDAP to gain political power created out of necessity the political soldier. The years 1920–23 were not only years in which the party strove to attain power and influence among the people, but were also years in which the Communists and others resorted more and more to brutal and violent tactics in their efforts to destroy the NSDAP and its ideals. The only method available to counter such political terror was the formation of well-trained and determined party members into a territorial force at all times ready and able to protect party meetings and, using the necessary muscle, eject anyone attempting to disturb the peace, terrorise the streets or take pleasure in similar violent activities.

On the eve of 4 November 1921, the Communists attempted to break up a meeting of the Führer's that was being held at the Hofbräuhaus in Munich, by way of a violent and provoked attack on the people attending. Forty-six brave and determined men beat off eight hundred Communists, eventually banishing every single one from the hall. On that same evening, when peace was restored, the Führer bestowed on these courageous fighters the title Sturmabteilung [Storm Troopers], and from this small band of founding members, there grew an army one million strong, tasked with the responsibility for overall national security in a country resolved to recapture its freedom.

From the very beginning, the Führer refused outright to consider the idea of secret operations or the foundation of clandestine troops. In his book Mein Kampf, he clearly described the tasks and responsibilities of the Sturmabteilung (SA). 'What we need are not one or two hundred bold conspirators,' he said, 'but many thousands of fanatical fighters totally dedicated to our aims and beliefs. We do not want to see one or two covert efforts at disorder, we need huge numbers of mass demonstrations openly and unmistakably supported by everyone. Our way ahead lies in the domination of the streets and not by cloak and dagger tactics,' he explained, 'We must show the Communists that today's master of the street is tomorrow's master of the nation, and that master is National Socialism.'

Within this framework, Adolf Hitler formed his first division of Storm Troopers, creating a politically orientated, formidable

Brown-shirted SA columns march past Hitler at the party rally in Nürnberg, November 1929

fighter, whose prime task was seen to be the defence of National Socialism and not military aggression.

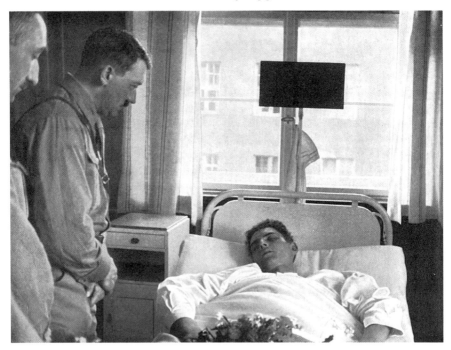

Hitler at the deathbed of a fallen SA member

The creation of such a revolutionary yet disciplined body popular amongst the people, soon necessitated its subdivision into regional groups, or 'Storms'; the name alone aptly expressing the task ahead. To storm the enemy, to wear him down to eventual destruction and thereby eradicate any further resistance to National Socialism was seen as the Storm Troopers' fundamental goal. Elderly heroes of the Great War combined with youthful brown-shirted warriors resulted in a movement of zealous loyalty and fearless sacrifice. These men, with their comradeship and frenzied belief in the political cause, soon became the hallmark of party union and unrivalled obedience. No assembly protected by men of the Sturmabteilung *was ever broken up, and no march by* Sturmabteilung *troopers ever failed to reach its destination. Even when some of the Führer's followers lay dead or injured, there never stood a coward in the Führer's ranks. From the blazing heat of summer to the bitter cold of winter, the Storm Troopers remained at constant readiness to heed the call of National Socialism, and if combat was involved, the longer it lasted, the surer it was of success. Despite the likelihood of losing one's life, or certainly one's livelihood, more and more volunteers came forward to join the ranks of the Storm Troopers. Old soldiers, young students, farmers, labourers, even civil servants, all queued to join, knowing that whosoever wore a brown shirt would never have need to take it off again. Within a few months, there wasn't a party demonstration, political march or election campaign meeting at which Hitler's Storm Troopers were not seen in attendance. It was also the brown- and black-capped* Sturmabteilung *that gave the nation its immortal anthem,* Die Fahne Hoch [Up with the Flag], *and matched by the Führer's own slogan, 'An idea is only worth as much as it finds men prepared to die for it'.*

[It is interesting to see how they became known as the Brown-shirts. In March 1919, General Paul von Lettow returned to Germany with his columns of soldiers from German East Africa, the only undefeated German unit of the First World War. Their uniform was of a brown, desert-like hue, and a large consignment that had failed to be dispatched in the closing days of the war was found some ten years later lying in a store in Germany. The discovery provided an immediate answer to the problems of uniforms in the early days of the *Sturmabteilung*, when funds were almost non-existent.]

On 30 January 1932, a fearsome battle took place in which some 400 party comrades paid for victory with their lives, and following which, a lantern procession of Storm Trooper divisions marched past Adolf Hitler for several hours. Previous years had been similarly difficult for the Sturmabteilung. *Their political enemies were not only very often of superior strength, but by then had also acquired considerably more sophisticated weaponry, including daggers and revolvers.*

A further adversary lay in the Bolsheviks, who, in their pursuit of an outdated administration, had stripped the troopers of their brown shirts. Not to be outdone, however, they then marched in white ones, and when they too were banned, they marched bare-breasted. They lost their jobs, they half starved, but they continued to fight for National Socialism, and even when ending up in prison, they were heard singing songs of freedom — freedom of the mind in the confines of a cell.

When their enemies tried sowing seeds of discontent and mistrust in their ranks, they reacted by moving even closer

77

When the government declared the Brown-shirts illegal, the men paraded shirtless

Columns of *Sturmabteilung* bearing their troop banners march past at the party congress, Nürnberg, 1933

78

together, giving the Führer even more support than before. Despite remaining unarmed, they continued to battle for mastery of the streets, often having to pay the price of death for their victories. With this task hardly completed, the conflict of January 1932 was the first in a new wave of extreme terror in street violence. This time, there was no lull in the fighting or pause to regroup, it was one endless headlong battle with many troopers not seeing a bed for many days.

The Bolshevicks, eventually retreating from the face of action and returning to their various hiding-places, had, however, not given up the struggle. With state elections just around the corner, the Storm Troopers soon gained the upper hand, though, and reverted to their guardianship of law and order, raiding the hiding-places and dragging away all remaining political agitators, Communists and persons dedicated to overthrowing the new Reich.

Spectacular parade of the *Sturmabteilung*, held at the Brandenburg Gate, Berlin, in 1933

Thereafter, hundreds of loyal supporters had to be taken out of the Sturmabteilung *and* Schutzstaffel *service in order to provide an administrative staff for the new state government. This initially left many open gaps in the ranks, but they were eventually filled by further courageous young volunteers devoted, to a man, to the great goal of National Socialism. Once again, hardly a meeting or demonstration took place without the brown- or black-shirted troops of law and order being present, with even the control of street traffic soon becoming another*

Together with Nazi Party Deputy Leader Rudolf Hess and party Treasurer, Franz Schwarz, Hitler attends a rally of SA comrades, Berlin, 1933

responsibility vested in the newly formed motorised units of the Sturmabteilung, *known as the* Nationalsozialistische Kraftfahr Korps, *or the NSKK. They too were always at hand whenever needed. Should an important road become blocked with snow, the NSKK would soon be on the spot shovelling it away, or following a heavy storm when towns and villages were flooded, the NSKK together with their colleagues of the SA, would be there doing all they could to help. Where security was at stake, it would be the turn of the* Schutzstaffel, *the SS to provide assistance, and when collections were held to raise funds or distribute clothes, everyone was there to help with the work.*

Overall, little had changed since the earliest days of the party. Uniforms and equipment had all to be paid for by the members themselves, and despite having to earn their daily bread, they were always ready to perform their duties with calm and professionalism whenever needed. With new problems constantly confronting them, the only privilege that SA members had was the knowledge that they were the founding souls of the Third Reich, the greatest Reich that Germany had ever known.

Not only did these gallant men face the responsibility of rescuing a nation and securing its internal safety, but they also had the task of recording day-to-day events that would become

Hitler takes the salute at a march past of his *Sturmabteilung*, Nürnberg, 1935

the new nation's history, at the same time ensuring that this record remained free from distortion and mistruth. This enormous work was carried out mostly by the Schutzstaffel, *the SS, whilst the SA continued the no less important task of the nation's daily affairs, known as the* Tägliche Kleinarbeit. *Both organisations were guardians of all that Germany and the German people held dear, in turn handing on their enormous success to the younger generations of front-line party comrades. In the same way that any soldier swears an oath of allegiance to protect his country against national and international adversaries, so too did each and every member of the SA and SS swear to defend the idea of National Socialism and carry its ideals throughout the coming decades. Whether military or political soldiers, they were soldiers of similar fortune and beliefs, soldiers of the Führer and the German Reich. When Adolf Hitler's divisions of soldiers paraded at the Nazi Party convention in Nürnberg in 1935, the entire nation proudly accepted these men as the nation's guardians of National Socialism, yesterday, today, and in a hundred years' time. Should their task see change in the coming years, their spirit would ever more hold fast to the nation's ideals, as did the spirits of those 46 gallant*

Treasurer Franz Schwarz, Deputy Leader Rudolf Hess and Labour front leader Robert Ley

men who stood by to defend our Führer, Adolf Hitler, on that fateful day at the Munich Hofbräuhaus in November 1923.

[This translation lumps together the formation and purpose of both the *Sturmabteilung* (SA) and the *Schutzstaffel* (SS) under one hat. In point of fact, the two organisations were vastly different. The SA was indeed formed on the night of 4 November 1921, by Adolf Hitler himself, to counter the terrorist and subversive tactics of the Communists and others. Under the leadership of Hitler's old compatriot Ernst Röhm, it grew to be a force of more than four million by the end of 1933, by which time its seemingly endless expansion had begun to concern many Reichswehr (Army) generals and leading party members. In June 1934, the entire body of the SA was ordered to take a month's leave. Within a few days, Röhm was imprisoned at Stadelheim gaol near Munich and was executed two days later. With the demise of its leader, the organisation soon fell into disrepute, culminating by the end of that year in the loss of all political and party function.

The black-shirted SS, on the other hand, was not formed until four years later, and then as a highly trained and well-armed personal bodyguard of Adolf Hitler. With notions and ideals differing vastly from those of Ernst Röhm, Heinrich Himmler led the establishment, together with its secret police wing, the Gestapo, and its élite combat battalion, the Waffen SS, from a small body of 200 men to an all-embracing empire within the Nazi state, totally eclipsing its elder cousin, the SA.]

SS Führer Heinreich Himmler, in company with the most senior officers of the *Schutzstaffel*

83

4

THE TIDE TURNS

If those who played a part in bringing the name of Adolf Hitler to the hearts of the German people could be likened to the members of an orchestra, then the conductor must surely be none other than Alfred Hugenberg.

Hugenberg began his spectacular business career as a director of Krupp Heavy Industries, rising in 1909 to be its chairman when still only 44 years of age. Along his path he acquired a huge newspaper empire, and with it a controlling interest in Germany's largest film studios, thereby managing to mobilise the opinions of the nation's middle classes against the Weimar constitution and all it stood for. In siding with Adolf Hitler and preaching similar conservative

Hitler attending a party rally in Brunswick, 1931

principles, he actively helped to put the Nazis in power, whilst at the same time greatly expanding his own economic profile. He led a group of Rhineland industrialists into the formation of a separate nationalist movement, violently anti-socialist and violently anti-government. After five years as chairman of his *Deutsche Nationale Volkspartei* (German National Peoples Party), he agreed to its disbandment and alliance to the Nazis, thereby for the first time placing his huge propaganda machine fully at Hitler's disposal.

In 1928, elections for the German Reichstag were held for the first time since Hitler had re-established himself as leader of the Nazi Party, and as a symbol of hope for many

84

people. He secured less than a million votes, resulting in only 12 seats out of the full Reichstag of 491.

A year later, Foreign Minister Gustav Stresemann died, and within a few days a crisis on Wall Street brought about an alarming recession and an urgent need to recover the gold that America had invested in Germany. By the summer of 1930, the nation's unemployed had risen to three million and Hitler was quick to seize the opportunity to attribute blame on the Jewish community and the Weimar government.

Adolf Hitler is greeted as he arrives for the Nazi Party congress in Nürnberg, March 1929

The same year saw the collapse of one of Germany's major banking houses, soon to be followed by Great Britain going off the gold standard and Japan marching into Manchuria, thereby threatening the very heart of world peace as established in the League of Nations. Misery, intrigue, unemployment and agony hit Germany in the years of 1931–32. Farms could no longer operate, the wheels of industry had ground to a standstill and, by the end of 1932, unemployment had reached the colossal level of seven million. A year later, President Hindenburg's term of office came to an end and he stood for re-election, but by now much of

85

Germany was infected with total hatred of Heinrich Brüning's Weimar government and the chaos it had brought. Hitler decided that he would stand as a candidate for the presidency, but as an Austrian he still had to acquire German citizenship. This was cunningly arranged for him in the small state of Brunswick, where the Nazis already held a popular majority. The ageing Hindenburg won 18½ million votes to Hitler's impressive 11 million, but by German constitutional law presidential elections required an overall two-thirds absolute majority, and this Hindenburg had failed to achieve. Elections were therefore held again, and this time Hitler scored 13 million, and it became clear to the world that he was a man of destiny in Germany.

Also at this time, the need arose for the Nazi Party to move its offices once again, this time to its final headquarters at Number 45 Briennerstrasse, a palatial private house until rebuilt by Hitler's favourite architect, Paul Ludwig Troost. It was opened on New Year's Day, 1931.

Hitler leaving the new party headquarters building, The Brown House, soon after its opening in January 1931

THE BROWN HOUSE

From works by Heinrich Hoffmann, 1933.

As National Socialism grew, so also did the need for a true party identity, a wise leadership, and above all else, a settled location to be seen publicly as the centre of party affairs.

Within a few years, membership had passed the one million mark, with the result that registration cards and filing cabinets could no longer be tucked away in backstreet pubs, and provisions had to be made for the future.

The Führer decided that the National Socialist movement must have a home of its own, and finding an attractive old town house in one of Munich's more elegant streets, he set about converting it into the party's central administrative headquarters.

Number 45 Briennerstrasse. The Nazi Party headquarters in 1931, which became known as The Brown House

Simple in appearance, it was given a tasteful renovation in which great care was taken to retain its unique and artistic character and, not forgetting Hitler's earlier dream of becoming an architect, he himself chose all the furnishings and fittings, and personally oversaw all the work on the splendid edifice.

The party's home became known as The Brown House, and its attractive appearance set a pattern for all restoration work in the years to come. The left-wing press, however, seized upon the opportunity to print cowardly reports of golden banisters, extravagant Persian carpets costing thousands of marks, and even that Adolf Hitler's own chambers were decorated in the most lavish oriental style. They wrote about secret lifts between the walls with concealed hiding-places full of weapons, and hosts of other fantasies besides. They were obviously reflecting on their own party comrades' shameful excesses, whose illicit dealings were well known to have financed numerous opulent villas.

[Notwithstanding the fact that such reports were in all probability highly exaggerated, the restoration work was a very expensive undertaking, and could not have been achieved without massive donation of funds, mostly from wealthy middle-class industrialists like Emil Kirdorf, who ran the 'Ruhr Treasury', a vast protection agency, and Fritz Thyssen of the United Steel Trust, author of the book *I Funded Hitler.*]

The Führer laughed aloud at their accusations, whilst his colleagues were equally amused at the disappointed visitors finding only polished floors and iron stairways. The three-storey building was proudly adorned on both sides of the entrance with the new national emblem, whilst in the middle of the reception hall stood a fine bust of Bismarck, surrounded by an array of party flags and banners. These had often to be removed, and usually at very short notice, when the police decided to spring one of their surprise investigations, but despite the odd anxious moment, they never managed to confiscate any of the party's belongings.

On the first floor stood the bronze bust of Dietrich Eckart, the deceased pioneer of National Socialism, close friend and mentor of Adolf Hitler. [Eckart is worth mentioning here, as he was truly the spiritual godfather of National Socialism. It was he who introduced Hitler to Munich society, taught him what social graces he possessed and groomed him for the role of Messiah. Together they wrote the book *Bolshevism from Moses to Lenin,* published in Munich in 1923, promulgating the belief that Jews were the occult power of revolutionary subversion and responsible for diverting mankind from his ordered path. Eckart exercised a remarkable personal influence over Hitler, who looked up to him as his counsellor and father figure, and to whom not surprisingly, he dedicated his work *Mein Kampf.*

Hitler's private study,
in The Brown House

Bust of Bismarck
and Nazi Party banners

Eckart was briefly imprisoned after the 1923 Beerhall Putsch, but died of heart failure shortly after his release.]

Also on the first floor, at the entrance to the room known as the 'Hall of Fame', stood a fine bronze plaque decorated with gold-plated laurel wreaths, and inscribed with the names of all the gallant men killed in action on 9 November 1923. Every time the Führer passed the plaque, he stopped for a brief moment in remembrance of his fallen comrades.

In the basement cafeteria, the staff and SA guards would often assemble to listen to the loudspeakers broadcasting election results or other party news. Many a time the Führer himself would join the assembly, talk with those present, or meet excited young girls and boys who had come to see their beloved Führer. Apart from the reception hall, on the ground floor were also the main records office, party treasurer Franz Schwarz and his offices, various filing rooms and typists' pool. On the first floor were the private chambers of the Führer, his adjutant, Fritz Brückner, Private Secretary, and later on, his deputy Rudolf Hess. Rooms were also allocated to the Sturmabteilung, *to the political faction of the party, and to his own personal staff.*

89

Hitler and his private secretary

Located on the second floor were the legal section, the press section and the very active propaganda department, which grew so large that it soon had to be moved to occupy the third floor

90

The Nazi party main records office, in The Brown House

The march from The Brown House to the Feldherrnhalle, 1934, in memory of comrades who fell on 9 November 1923

91

on its own. Finally, the attic floor housed the party archives, along with various technical and administrative offices.

This very impressive and beautiful building soon symbolised the strength and determination of National Socialism to both the German people and to the party's enemies alike. The post office was quick to learn that 'The Brown House' was address enough for Number 45 Briennerstrasse, an address which was to become soul sacred for millions of people.

On the summit of the Obersalzburg, the Führer often walked and dreamed of the future, but in The Brown House such dreams became a reality.

With the population now evenly split between Hindenburg and Hitler, national hysteria and near civil war broke out. Communists and Nazis were fighting each other daily in the streets, whilst in government, confused intrigue and desperate manoeuvring undermined the entire stability of German sovereignty.

Hitler loved to address young people. He is seen here talking with SA members in the basement canteen at party headquarters

In May 1932, a Nazi Party march into the known Communist quarter of Hamburg called Kleine Freiheit, resulted in 19 dead and 285 wounded. Hindenburg had already replaced the much-loathed Chancellor Brüning by the more popular Chairman of the Catholic Centre Party and known advocate of the Hohenzollern monarchy, Franz von Papen, and now this latest brawl was the excuse he needed for dismissing the entire cabinet as incompetent and incapable.

In July 1932 the complicated German political machine once again called the people to the polls, resulting this time in a massive Nazi gain of nearly 14 million votes, or 230 seats (37 per cent) in the Reichstag. When parliament resat a month later, the anti-government faction of Nazis, Communists and, with great folly, the Social Democrats, combined to throw out von Papen, who in retaliation dissolved the house and again appealed to the electorate.

This time, largely through lack of funds, the Nazis lost ground, securing only 196 seats, but by now the democratic principle of proportional representation had begun to crumble. More intrigue and undercover terrorism threatened Hindenburg's administration, resulting in his decision to rule Germany by presidential decree with military support.

Surviving old comrades of the 9 November putsch stand in memory of lost companions, 1935

The man largely responsible for the appointment and dismissal of both Brüning and von Papen as Reichschancellors, one General Kurt von Schleicher, was himself now appointed by Hindenburg as Germany's last Chancellor of the Weimar era. As a young subaltern von Schleicher had served in the President's own regiment, the Third Foot Guards, and throughout his fine military career he had remained a close personal friend of Hindenburg. He became closely involved with the politics of the nation during his period as head of press and public affairs in the Ministry of Defence, and from this appointment he emerged as a talented and unscrupulous schemer. Whilst Germany's electoral machinery ground more and more to a standstill, Hindenburg had great need

Nazi Party election campaign poster

of von Schleicher's advice. However, his chancellorship lasted a mere 57 days, in turn brought down, in yet another web of intrigue, by von Papen, the very man he had replaced.

On further advice from von Papen, Hindenburg now accepted the Nazis as the strongest arm of the coalition, and on that fateful day of 30 January 1933, he offered the post of Chancellor of Germany to Adolf Hitler.

Further Nazi Party campaign posters in the 1932 general elections

HITLER BECOMES CHANCELLOR OF GERMANY

From journals of the NSDAP Propaganda Department, 1935.

The year 1933 was known in Germany as the year of decision-making. Following a lengthy period of bitter strife and insecurity, it was the year in which the National Socialists began to take on a new and glorious identity, the end result of seven years' tireless effort by the organisation.

Chancellor Franz von Papen accompanies Adolf Hitler to a meeting with the President, Paul von Hindenburg, at which Hitler is offered the Chancellorship of Germany, 30 January 1933

The transformation began with a programme of massive campaigning for the state parliamentary elections in Lippe, Westfalen. Elements of the left-wing press seized the opportunity to mock the preparations being made by the National Socialists, accusing them of gross over-expenditure and ridiculous emphasis on such an insignificant occasion. In fact, the mockery of the election by the opposition made the public far more aware of the event, thereby attracting far more interest than would otherwise have been the case.

The election contest surpassed any propaganda exercise that the party could have wished for and, following a triumphal victory that quite shattered the opposition, swastika banners were openly paraded for the first time.

The Führer himself also took part in the front line by attending rallies up and down the country, speaking to the people as often as he could, not only in the big cities, but also in the smallest of villages where his name was still hardly known. During the 10-day Lippe campaign, 18 meetings were held in which the Führer was the main speaker, with the result that on polling day no fewer than 47.8 per cent of the electorate decided in favour of Adolf Hitler and National Socialism. A few days earlier, the left-wing press had stated that Hitler could not possibly expect anything more than 33 per cent of the vote. Even in such a small state as Lippe, this result began to shape the changing mood of the nation.

Having begun by mocking their campaign, the opposition then continued by mocking the result, but now, with such a clear signal as this election had shown, the people no longer listened to, much less believed, anything they had to say. On the day following this election, the Führer attended a rally in Weimar, the constitutional heart of Germany, where he addressed an assembly of some 10,000 SA soldiers. 'In the heart of Germany,' he said, 'we vow to fight until we achieve our goal, always remaining resolute and loyal to this national cause.'

On 21 January, the Berlin detachment of the SA marched to the Bülow Platz, and paraded in front of the Karl Liebknecht Haus. By now, Chancellor Schleicher, the last Chancellor of the Weimar Republic, stood very much alone. The entire farming community of Germany, completely fed up with the perpetual administrative disorder of the Weimar government, had gathered in the city, causing little less than total disarray, something the cabinet tried frantically to hush up but with little success. The crucial by-election at Lippe had been a testing

President von Hindenburg with Adolf Hitler, the new Chancellor of Germany

time for Hitler's vast election machinery, and following such overwhelming success, its wheels began turning at an even greater pace and with even greater conviction. Ideally, the Führer need only push a button and the entire election mechanism would roll into action wherever it was needed, and with a force never seen before.

Barely two weeks after the Lippe election, von Schleicher's cabinet began to crumble, and although Reichspresident von Hindenburg still refused to acknowledge the need for a new Chancellor, it was announced that national elections would be held in the following March.

Hitler opens Party Day in Nürnberg town hall, 1935

Adolf Hitler moved to tighten his grip on election fever by establishing a new headquarters in the Kaiserhof building, directly opposite the Imperial Chancellery. Here an ever-increasing crowd gathered day and night, calling up to Hitler's window and demanding an end to the burnt-out and powerless Weimar democracy, now fit only for the ashes.

100

On 28 January, President von Hindenburg ordered von Papen to form a government, but with so many ministers now jostling for a position in any new Hitler government, von Papen found it impossible to administer the nation. On the following Monday morning, 30 January, Adolf Hitler, accompanied by Franz von Papen, was summoned to the Chancellery, returning at noon as the new Chancellor of Germany, marking the greatest event yet in German history. With the support of van Papen as his deputy, and together with Hermann Göring, Franz Seldte, Wilhelm Frick and Alfred Hugenberg, Hitler very soon formed a new cabinet.

Hitler and von Hindenburg drive through Berlin

Neither the power of the press nor the speed of the wireless were as fast as the people who eagerly spread the joyous tidings of Adolf Hitler's appointment. Like a vast tidal wave, the news flashed from house to house and street to street, and soon the name of Adolf Hitler and his Chancellorship was carried by the people the length and breadth of Germany. An entire nation rejoiced at the knowledge that a new Reichschancellor had been appointed, and to a man, everyone knew what that meant for the country.

By the time that the newspapers were on the streets carrying the headline news, it wasn't news at all, but even so, every

101

In the days following his appointment as Chancellor, Hitler was often seen in the company of the President

copy was enthusiastically snatched up. Everyone, everywhere, wanted to see every detail for themselves printed in black and white. Within a few hours, the account had been transmitted to every corner of the world by journalists, who hastily dispatched lengthy cables regardless of expenses, whilst in complete calm, the Führer and his government made preparations to take over the running of the nation. Further support was soon apparent in all the big cities, as people gathered, waving the victorious colours of the Great War, along with the new swastika-emblazoned banner of the country's future. In Berlin, thousands of cheering people, many of whom had never met before, embraced each other in the streets and lit each other's lanterns in the huge procession that made its way that night from the Unter den Linden, to the Wilhelmstrasse, the length of the city. The heart of the capital was a sea of joy, as thousands more

In the presence of the German President, Paul von Hindenburg, and an invited audience of senior government members, Adolf Hitler reads his declaration of a new constitution following his appointment as Chancellor of Germany, Potsdam, March 1933

All over the nation, people thronged to participate in the news

men, women and children joined the divisions of steel-helmeted soldiers in a candlelight celebration. Suddenly, a deafening cheer followed by thunderous applause was heard as there on the chancellery balcony stood the nation's heroes, the grand old Field Marshal, President of Germany Paul von Hindenburg, and

104

Lance-Corporal, now Reichschancellor, Adolf Hitler. As they stood together, acknowledging the love and admiration of all the people, they signified the rich history of the German nation and the future happiness and prosperity of its citizens. Words could not describe the excitement and splendour of the moment, and as evening gave way to nightfall, the volume of cheering and waving increased by the minute.

Hitler with his full cabinet, which he formed within a few days of becoming Reichschancellor of Germany

The appointment of Adolf Hitler as Chancellor, and the subsequent celebrations, were felt throughout Germany like a gigantic rock being lifted from the shoulders of the nation, or like the opening of a curtain that, for no less than 14 years, had darkened the lives of a race of people. This sudden liberation of an entire section of humanity resulted in the week-long cheering and acclaiming of those who had achieved the miracle, the Field Marshal and the Chancellor.

Not one soul who was present in Berlin that night can ever forget the overwhelming experience wherein an entire nation stood hand in hand, regardless of colour, class or intellect. The President and the Chancellor stood hour after hour on the *balcony of the Reichschancellery greeting the soldiers and the people, and yet, as tears of happiness flowed from so many faces and bouquets of flowers were thrown in the air, suddenly shots rang out in the small district of Charlottenburg. Sturmführer Maikowski and policemen Zarvik had been brutally assassinated, and Storm Troop 33 had lost one of its best men.*

Hitler casts his vote, Königsberg, 1933

5

A NATION REAWAKENS

It is sometimes thought abroad, and often claimed by the National Socialists, that Adolf Hitler was swept into power by a great mass movement. He was not. He was, in the end, jobbed into power by a group of right-wing politicians of the 'old gang', who despised the socialists, feared the Communists and thought that they could control him.

Following his appointment as Chancellor, Hitler moved swiftly to cement his position.

Hitler greeted by crowds of supporters and well-wishers

On 27 February 1933, less than one month after his sensational nomination to the Chancellorship, there occurred a scandalous

One nation

One people

One Führer

108

event, without doubt set up by the Nazis as a mammoth propaganda exercise, but which backfired badly, especially in its objectives overseas.

Hitler, accompanied by his trusty SS Standartenführer Schreck, driving in the country

As the sun rose, smoke and flames were seen pouring from the first floor of the Reichstag building, the German houses of parliament, leaving it little more than a charred shell by the same evening. Found wandering on the site, in a semi-comitose, half-naked state, was the young Dutch homosexual Marinus van der Lubbe. He was a bricklayer by trade, but had been unemployed for many months, and as an ardent anarchist had made one or two friends in the Berlin faction of the NSDAP. At the initial police interrogation he had confessed to being the sole instigator of the fire, but by the time the trial was brought before the Leipzig supreme court, the Nazi authorities had also arrested the Bulgarian Communist leader, Georgi Dimitrov, and others, accusing them of being behind the arson. Lubbe had also been found to be partially blind, thereby largely refuting the theory that he alone had fired the building. His apathetic, bewildered performance at his trial gave much credence to the thought that he had been drugged and manipulated by the Nazis.

The one remaining threat to the NSDAP was the Communist

organisation, and its removal from any degree of popularity had to be Hitler's prime objective if he was going to secure his position as leader of Germany.

Hitler determines the day's route

THE DAY OF THE AWAKENING NATION

From *Deutschland Erwacht, Germany Reawakens* by Obersturmführer Felix Albrecht.

On 1 February 1933, Adolf Hitler spoke on the German wireless for the first time. Everyone crowded around their sets, there wasn't a loudspeaker or headphone that wasn't being used that evening.

'The principal aim of the new government,' he said, 'is to erase the damage and memory of the last 14 years, by way of eliminating unemployment, creating an era of peace and freedom for the nation, and thereby work and bread for the people. To achieve this,' he continued, 'my government requires a time span of four years.'

The Führer

The immediate dissolution of the Reichstag was ordered, and elections arranged to allow the people free opportunity to voice their own approval. Clearly the Führer wanted them to make their own decision. 'Are you for me, or against me?' he said to the nation. 'Answer me now, without fear or reservation!' And indeed, the nation replied. On the eve of the elections, 5 March 1933, Dr Joseph Göbbels announced that the following day would for evermore be called 'The Day of the Awakening Nation', and truly the day lived up to its name.

As dusk fell, fires were lit all over Germany, and from the mountain peaks to the village streets, everyone could see them from their windows and declare with one voice their belief in Adolf Hitler and their

111

Hitler demonstrates his gift for public speaking

112

recognition of the swastika symbol, emblem of the new Reich. On the following day, 52 per cent of all the people of Germany voted in support of the new government, and this was seen by the whole world as truly an honestly contested election, within the democratic laws of the nation's constitution, with an unequivocal result.

A few days earlier, on 27 February, an unbelievable crime took place. The Reichstag building was set ablaze in an arson attempt that left most of it in ashes, believed to have been perpetrated by hideaway Bolsheviks. The Red Revolt was obviously still very much unchecked throughout the country, with rebellious acts of insurgence continually being reported. The stability of the new nation still teetered on a knife edge, but no longer was the ineffectual administration of the Weimar era in power.

The government took immediate steps to curb such unrest, and within a few days, the Bolsheviks had all retreated into their foxholes, from whence they emerged to stage this one final offensive. No stone was left unturned in the subsequent efforts to smoke out the rebels.

Such a monstrous crime found no sympathy amongst the German people, who to a man were outraged by the abhorrent act.

Hitler discusses the air route with his personal pilot, Captain Baur

Hitler speaks to the people following the burning of the Reichstag, February 1933

On 8 March, three days after the election, the Karl Liebnecht building, which had for many years been the headquarters of the Marxist movement, was finally taken over by the NSDAP, and swastika-emblazoned banners were proudly hoisted all around the rooftops, and within a few weeks, all remaining provincial governments and administrations had fallen to the flag of National Socialism. Even the state government of Bavaria had been swept away, so that from the mountains of the Alps to the shores of the North Sea the swastika emblem of the National Socialist German Workers Party could be seen to signal the new surge of political uprising and patriotic pride. In one quick strike, the government put down all resistance which could in any way have posed a threat to Germany's future and the unity of the German people.

The bright red swastika flag was also to be seen on all the graves of those dead heroes who had given their lives for the nation during both the Great War, and the revolutions that followed, finally establishing the undeniable fact that their sacrifice had not been in vain. In their honour, 12 March had been declared a national day of remembrance. It was a bright and sunny day as the nation gathered to mourn the loss of its departed heroes, but with the Reichstag building burned to the ground, the service of commemoration was held in the state opera house.

Shaking hands with a well-wisher

115

Chancellor Adolf Hitler
and President von
Hindenburg attend a
service of remembrance

By his own example, Hitler promotes air travel

In front of this masterpiece of Prussian architecture, the people waited for hours to see the grand old guard of the Imperial Army, together with the brown-coated SA and the black-uniformed troops of the SS, march past in remembrance. Students stood at the memorial entrance, where a golden wreath had been placed on an enormous stone monument, from where Reichspresident von Hindenburg was met by the Chancellor, Adolf Hitler, as he arrived for this most auspicious occasion. Orders were given, and with their steel-grey helmets gleaming in the brilliant sunlight, column after column of Germany's proud soldiers marched past their leaders in the grandest parade held since the Führer took office.

Everywhere people were seen waving flags of many different colours and designs. Most had the old standards of the nation's great regiments and the colours of the Imperial Guard, but many had already acquired the new red, white and black swastika standard of the new Reich, fast becoming recognised the world over.

Hitler's aircraft, D-2600, flying over the city of Nürnberg

117

Apart from the marching men, the military bands and the sea of waving flags, little else stirred in that great square, so awe-inspiring was the event. Then, as President von Hindenburg walked slowly up to the memorial to place his wreath at the foot, a hundred thousand hands rose in salute and admiration for the great and much loved man. He was followed in turn by Chancellor Adolf Hitler, who placed his own wreath alongside that of the President with such reverence that it was as if he feared that he might waken the sleeping heroes.

As both men turned to leave the square, there followed a tumultous cheer, and a wall of outstretched arms as people hoped to shake their hands. No longer could it be said that two million men had died in vain. The shame and guilt of a defeated nation now lay buried in the history books, and this new spirit that had rekindled the hearts and souls of German people would live for ever more. The glorious nation had become one Reich again, and at a solemn and moving ceremony in Potsdam, on the outskirts of Berlin, a few days later, this enactment of German sovereignty was ratified in perpetuity.

The swastika flag of the new Reich was to be seen as a flag of great honour and everlasting hope, symbolising the heroism and determination of that great nation. Never before had a day of mourning given a land and its people such strength and courage, for truly it was the dawn of a new era for Germany.

The trial of Leipzig was a world event, with over one hundred journalists attending from nearly as many nations. Dimitrov emerged as the central figure, turning the tables on his accusers and driving them very much on the defensive. He succeeded in reducing the Prussian Minister of State, Hermann Göring, to quivering rage. 'I didn't come here to be accused by you,' Göring shouted uncontrollably in court. 'As far as I am concerned, you are a rogue who should have been hanged long ago.' This irresponsible and offensive behaviour resulted in an official caution by the judges, and Göring was then forced to leave the courtroom and face a barrage of questions from the press outside.

Party rally in Weimar's historic market-place, 1932

The Communists were all acquitted, leaving only the unfortunate Lubbe holding the reins of guilt, and he was subsequently executed in the courtyard of Leipzig prison under a special retroactive law, known as the 'Lex van der Lubbe', initiated by the Nazis especially for the case. They refused to hand over his body to his family in Holland. The controversy over whether Lubbe acted alone or was indeed an unwilling victim of the Nazis continues to concern historians till today. The facts nowadays suggest that

119

Children always fascinated Hitler, although he had none himself

there was little doubt that the Nazis had planned the whole affair, in order to outlaw the Communists for all time.

Although the fire failed in its propaganda objectives abroad, it did produce results in Germany, further strengthening the hand of the Nazi Party. In March 1933, under conditions of tumult, mental stress and tremendous National Socialist propaganda, the German people elected a new Reichstag. Even now, Hitler only obtained 43.9 per cent of the votes cast, giving him 288 seats in parliament. The majority of his votes had come either from the frontier districts where nationalist sentiments were rife, or from localities of small farmers who were bitterly resentful of a government which had forced them to sell out by auction in order to survive. That same month, Hitler managed to bring before parliament an outrageous hoax called the enabling law, which would permit him, whenever necessary, powers beyond the government, apparently for the maintenance of law and order in the country. With the house packed full of brown-shirted Nazi members and Storm Troopers everywhere in the streets, it was no surprise that the motion was carried by a vote of 441 to 94.

The passing of this law, the very last democratic debate held in the German parliament until the end of the Third Reich, gave Adolf Hitler what he truly wanted, his licence as a dictator.

The SA show their muscle in Leipzig, at the time of the trial of Marinus van der Lubbe. Behind the Führer is the Nazi Governor of Saxony, Helmut Mutschmann

DEVELOPMENTS IN GERMANY, FOLLOWING HITLER'S SEIZURE OF POWER

From journals of the NSDAP Propaganda Department, 1935.

Many political and social advances were made during the year 1933, but three noteworthy events bear particular mention. First, the visit of Adolf Hitler to the navy to witness fleet manoeuvres in the bay of Kiel; second, the national display of gymnastics in Stuttgart; and third, the birth of the Reichsautobahn network, held at a stirring ceremony on the outskirts of the city of Frankfurt.

Hitler lays the foundation of the *Autobahn* system, Frankfurt, 1933

122

This was not the first time Adolf Hitler had been a guest of the German navy. In 1932 he had visited Kiel, and spent a short period of time aboard the Cruiser Köln, although at that time only as a private individual, albeit a struggling political leader.

Hardly a year later, he now returned as Chancellor of Germany and founder of a new era in the nation's history.

Admiral Räder accompanies Hitler on his visit to the German navy, Kiel, 1933

He arrived in Kiel by aeroplane, and whilst circling over the city was clearly able to see the fleet below, and the state it was in. There lay a few old cruisers, one or two torpedo boats, a destroyer and that was about all. There were no submarines, no battleships, for the Treaty of Versailles had expressly forbidden the possession of such vessels. 'Destroy the ships it might have done,' he thought, 'but never the men, whose courage had risen above the mutiny of 1918, and the consequent establishment of the Weimar Republic.' As his aircraft made its approach to land, Adolf Hitler proudly imagined great fleets of battleships, submarines even aircraft-carriers, and all in the colours of the new German Reich. Accompanied by his Reichsminister for Propaganda, Dr Joseph Göbbels, his ministers for war, aviation and the SS, the Führer stepped aboard the old cruiser Emden,

123

to a warm welcome from Admiral Räder, the head of the navy, and a rousing cheer from men of the ship's company. Keen to show what the navy could still manage, the men were soon at their action stations, and in impeccable order the warships steamed in line ahead, out of the bay.

The Führer found that the cool sea air did him a power of good, and with his hair blowing in the wind, he keenly followed the fleet manoeuvres. Memories came flooding back, of Admiral Spee's lonely vigil at the Falklands Islands, and of the battle of the Skagerrak, which, despite Germany failing to dispatch anything like sufficient numbers of ships, could still be

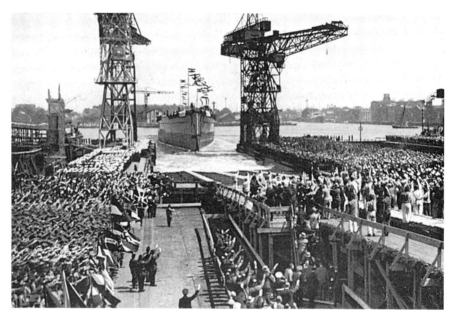

One of the first ships to be launched in the new building programme was the pocket battleship *Admiral Graf Spee*

considered a resounding victory. He recalled the warship Gödm and its heroic battle at the Dardenelles, and the U-boat flotilla, of which very few ever returned. He particularly remembered the submarine Deutschland, which alone broke through the enemy's blockade in the Channel and crossed the Atlantic to carry out many successful raids on enemy shipping along the coasts of America. With remorse and sadness, he recalled the terrible days of the Kiel mutiny, when here in this very spot, Bolshevik *revolutionaries with their red flags flying had attempted to stir up rebellious sentiment throughout the navy. It was appropriate, he thought, that his first visit as Chancellor of Germany should be in the very place where this Communist uprising had originated. 'Such a shameful act must never be allowed to happen again,' he thought, and in his mind he saw the new navy of the German Reich, a National Socialist navy, and carrying with it the same spirit in its heart that the British had shown at Scapa Flow, and from which he knew they had never been known to falter.*

Hitler never missed an opportunity to talk to the German workers. Here he is with the men building the cruiser *Admiral Hipper* in Hamburg

As the great day sadly came to an end, in turn each ship steamed past the Emden, *with the crews of each giving three tumultous cheers and the Führer proudly replying with outstretched arms in salute. As he came to leave the ship, he was surrounded by all the officers, shaking hands and again raising thunderous applause which could be heard right across the harbour of Kiel. That day, a new fleet of ships, indeed a new navy for the Third Reich, had been born.*

The National Gymnastics Festival was held at the Camstatter Park, near Stuttgart. Thousands of gymnasts, both men and women, and all dressed in gleaming white, paraded at the opening ceremony, with each one proudly recalling the words of Adolf Hitler in his work Mein Kampf *that in the training of the mind, the needs of the body must not be overlooked. It must be coached, drilled and disciplined so as to achieve a peak of performance and thereby a readiness for distinction when called upon to act.*

Accompanied by party Deputy Leader Rudolf Hess and Minister for Youth and Sports Baldur von Shirach, Hitler reviews the participants at the National Gymnastics Festival in Stuttgart, 1933

No one before had so clearly defined the need for healthy sports and gymnastics as Adolf Hitler. The day had been a celebration of bodily beauty and great acheivement, a day in which the best of the nation and the beauty of its race had been shown off to the world.

Once again, the Führer was greeted with tremendous accord, with cries of 'Heil Hitler' echoing around the stadium, and as the competition unfolded, Adolf Hitler clearly saw the magnificent way in which the gymnasts had mastered their various skills, and in the displays, he saw the perfect outward and visible signs of the nation's inward and spiritual political will, and furthermore, the constant need for National Socialism to be uppermost in the eyes of the people. In their individual successes, he perceived the triumph of a nation now quite ready to defend its own at the forthcoming Olympic Games, to be hosted in four years' time here in Germany. 'It must be the most splendid games ever held,' he thought, 'and most worthy of a National Socialist Reich, and the young team that would carry away so many gold awards.'

That was all very clear, as he stood and watched the fine gymnasts that day at Camstatter Park.

More young well-wishers

127

On 23 September 1933, the Führer sank his spade into the earth near a little village on the outskirts of Frankfurt, and a new age of surface transport was born. The Reichsautobahn programme, soon to be known as the roads of the Führer, was an immense undertaking. At the time, only a few people could visualise the enormity of the task, but within a few years every nation in the world would discover that with such magnificent highways, Germany had evolved the most beautiful and efficient road network ever to be seen. From Hamburg to Basel, from Stettin to Munich, from Aachen to Breslau and from Saarbrücken to Berlin, the web of this gigantic project spread across the Reich, opening the doors of travel to all the people, thereby making it easier and safer to drive to the four corners of the nation.

Hitler visits the works of Bayrischen Motorenwerken (BMW)

Without the interruptions of crossroads or intersections, the Führer's roads could now be likened to the political determination of the National Socialist Reich. The undertaking of the century began in Frankfurt on that September day, and what the construction of the railways meant to the nineteenth century, the building of the autobahn meant to the twentieth. Freight, which earlier had had to be reloaded three or four times during the course of one journey, could now be transported on the autobahn

128

direct from factory to consumer without any delay. Furthermore, the country roads were no longer faced with destruction by heavy trucks, and people were no longer disturbed at night by the endless roll of vehicles through the villages.

As the autobahn separated opposing traffic in different lanes, the private individual could now drive for many hours in complete safety, and both quicker and cheaper. Faster travel also dictated the need for higher-quality cars, with better design for improved speed, greater comfort and firmer road-holding especially in wet and windy conditions. Last but not least, the enormity of the project provided much-needed labour for thousands of men. Above all else, the autobahn programme was responsible for the rapid development in Germany, following Adolf Hitler's rise to the Chancellorship. New towns grew up near the autobahn intersections, in the same way that cities had first appeared at railway junctions a century earlier.

After inaugurating the *autobahn* programme, Hitler had an intense interest in improved motor car design. Here he is visiting the Mercedes stand at the 1935 International Motor Exhibition in Berlin

Despite the fleeting changes that occurred during Hitler's first few years in power, he continually emphasised the need to hold fast to Germany's illustrious past. During the party's 14-year

129

struggle, the nation had stood still, but with the demise of the Weimar constitution, history was on the move once again, and the NSDAP soon made up for the years of bloodshed and betrayal.

Soon after Adolf Hitler's take-over of Germany, the Reichsminister for Aviation, Hermann Göring, decided to name the largest and quite the most beautiful flying machine the world had ever known the Hindenburg, after the nation's great President and hero. Like the man himself, the airship was enormously strong and immensely powerful, a true masterpiece of German engineering. It bore the colours of the Third Reich, and the swastika emblem on the tail, a symbol of the nation's industrial and financial recovery. It flew across countries and continents, seas and oceans, and all in the cause of peaceful communication for the communities of the world. Its creation was a tribute to Germany's love of global peace and goodwill, and a reminder to the world of the nation's pride and technical excellence.

Hitler is proudly shown the Mercedes racing car by the Daimler Benz management

On the anniversary of the Battle of Tannenberg, a large commemorative ceremony was held in the province of East Prussia. Attended by members of the Reichsgovernment and

130

officials from various state administrations, together with detachments from the SA and the SS, army units in their new uniforms and steel helmets and thousands of civilians, the occasion paid honour to the nation's most decorated military commander, Field Marshal Hindenburg, who 19 years previously had fought so triumphantly in order to defend Germany's soil. Continuing to symbolise the solidarity of the Prussian people and their destiny in the new German Reich, Field Marshal Hindenburg proudly stood to take the salute at the military march past, after which he was bedecked with flowers and given a tumultous send-off by the crowds of spectators.

Scarcely had the Field Marshal left the scene when the Führer also departed by aeroplane, in order to attend another party rally in the Saar district of southern Germany.

Day after day he travelled to every corner of the country to

A Nazi Party rally in Frankfurt

meet and speak to the people, thereby uniting the power of National Socialism with the future of Germany's Third Reich. With his dynamic personality and outstanding vision, he constantly reminded the community of their proud history and their challenging future, and whenever he spoke, he was hailed by all as the protector of the nation and the guardian of hope for its citizens.

131

The Nazi election campaign had been based on bluster, threats and appeals to prejudice and hatred, with street battles against Communists and other political opponents being the party's stock-in-trade. Now that the Nazis were in power, all the evil heritage of the years of hatred and bigotry was let loose.

Hitler visits President von Hindenburg for the last time, at the end of July 1934

Hitler is met by Minister Richard Darre, June 1933, on the occasion of his appointment as Minister of Food and Agriculture, and at the same time, SS General in charge of the SS Race and Resettlement Bureau. It was Darre's ideas of selective breeding that inspired Himmler to create a master race within the ranks of the SS

With no pretence at legal procedure, squads of *Sturmabteilung* beat up socialists, trade unionists and anyone else whose political views ran counter to those now in power. In the state of Prussia, Göring had already established the secret police, the Gestapo, whose lawless actions filled the hearts and minds of the people with fear and despair. Within a few months, the concentration camps were filling up not only with criminals, but mostly with people whose utterances simply did not suit Nazi doctrine.

In May 1933, all trade unions in Germany were dissolved, to be followed two months later by all political parties except, of course, for the National Socialists, or Nazis. At the same time, laws had been passed preventing all those of Jewish descent from holding public office, then, quickly throwing off any mask of legality, the Nazis proceeded to govern the country by their own horrible standards. The terrible page in human history grew even grimmer, culminating on 30 June 1934 in the 'Night of the Long Knives'. In one mass murder, Hitler swept away all those who might still have posed a challenge to his leadership.

Altogether, 77 leading Nazis, and 110 others were brutally executed that night, including such names as Gregor Strasser, who first brought the Nazi movement to northern Germany, General von Schleicher and his wife, and even Hitler's close colleague and one-time commander of the Storm Troopers, Ernst Röhm.

Hitler at the time of President von Hindenburg's death

On 2 August 1934, President von Hindenburg died, and this time there was no election. Hitler announced his intention of combining in his own person the office of President and that of Chancellor.

One organisation, the *Wehrmacht* (German army), still remained not entirely controlled by Hitler. Until the passing of the Enabling Law in May 1933, Hitler's rule had, outwardly at least, always seemed constitutional, and after that date whatever other ideas or motives his generals might have had, his policy of rearmament coincided

134

with their own interest. Further-more, for his first few years in power he openly encouraged the old army and the new Nazi movement to walk side by side, but he never allowed anyone to actually share power with him.

However, by the end of 1937, he felt strong enough to strike at the military, and on a disgraceful trumped-up charge of homosexual indecency, General Werner von Fritsch, the chief of the German High Command, and 16 other senior officers, were dismissed from their posts. In von Fritsch's court martial, Heinrich Himmler produced a notorious male prostitute, Hans Schmidt, whose false testimony convinced Hitler that the charges were true. Hitler himself then assumed the position of supreme commander of the Wehrmacht, appointing as his deputy the chief of staff General Wilhelm Keitel, whom he knew would do as he was told.

Keitel was promoted Field Marshal after negotiating the French surrender in 1940. He served Hitler with absolute loyalty, continuing to the very last under the Dönitz government in May 1945, organising the surrender of the German army before his arrest by the allies. His subservience to Hitler became a byword in the army, where he was known as Lakeitel, or Lackey Keitel. It was his 'Nacht und Nebel' policy (killings without trial – literally night and fog) that led to his inclusion among the major war criminals, and was sentenced to death by hanging at Nürnberg on 16 October 1946.

The complicated history of the years between 1934 and 1939 is closely linked to Western European politics, and was a time of continuing pressure on the German population by the Nazi regime.

The Führer with his military commanders, before the purge in 1937
(left to right, Adolf Hitler, Reichsmarschall Hermann Göring, Field Marshal Werner von Blomberg, General Werner von Fritsch, Grand Admiral Erich Räder)

135

Hitler reviews a parade of soldiers outside the Kaiserpfalz building, Goslar, 1934

THE HITLER YOUTH MOVEMENT

A personal report by Reich Youth Leader Baldur von Shirach.

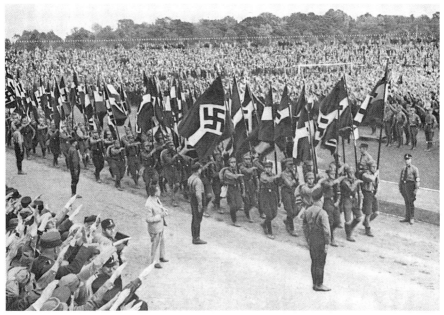

An early photograph of the young Hitler Youth movement on parade, Potsdam, 1932

The Hitler Youth was established as early as 1925, in the Prussian town of Planen-Vogtland, initially as an offshoot of the Sturmabteilung *and with the purpose of directing the youthful spirit of Germany towards Adolf Hitler and his new ideology. In taking the oath of allegiance to the Führer, every young person vowed to uphold the honour and true meaning of National Socialism, and follow a life of courage and devoted servitude. Compared to the earlier German youth movement known as the Bird of Passage Organisation, which was similar in principle and dedicated from the outset towards public service, the Führer's youth movement embraced the logical concept of 'Hitler thought', with total devotion to authority and unfailing discipline as hallmarks of successful progress.*

At the age of ten years, a youngster could already expect to join the Jungvolk *[the Young People], an ambitious brigade of boys and girls serving as the youngest guardians of National Socialism. At the age of fourteen, a boy transferred to the Hitler*

137

Youth itself, whilst his sister became a member of the Bund Deutscher Mädel, *the national organisation for girls of German nationality, an independent community within the framework of the Hitler Youth movement.*

[Incidentally, von Schirach was only half German, having an American mother, and being the grandson of a soldier who lost his leg in the Battle of Bull Run, Virginia, in August 1862. Mystery often surrounds his appointment as Reich Youth Leader, one possible explanation being that his wife, a well-noted beauty, was rumoured to be Hitler's mistress during the early period of the Nazi movement. He was arrested in 1945 and stood trial as a Nazi war criminal at Nürnberg, but was sentenced to only 20 years' imprisonment, due to his children's love of America. He died in 1974.]

Following the example of its political mentor, Adolf Hitler, the organisation adopted as its principal task the continued elimination of Marxist elements and the eradication of all forces contrary in opinion to the principles of National Socialism. Firmly believing in the values of community spirit rather than the single mind, the Hitler Youth was from its very beginning designed to defend itself against the forces of evil in any quarter of the globe. Its revolutionary attitude was seen not only

A Hitler Youth member presents flowers to President von Hindenburg, Labour Day, May 1933

The Führer shares some bad news. A Hitler Youth boy shows Adolf Hitler a letter from his sick mother

138

The Reich Youth Leader, Baldur von Schirach, accompanies the Führer to a Hitler Youth jamboree in Nürnberg, 1934

in the rejection of all things past and present, but in the very creation of new ideals and expressions so necessary in the foundation of National Socialism.

Responsible to the Führer for this very important branch of the NSDAP and its constituent societies was the Reich Youth Leader, Baldur von Schirach, with his headquarters at the Reich Jugend Führung *in Potsdam. As leader of the organisation and professor in all matters of political and cultural learning, the primary task of the Reich Youth Leader was to pass on the ideas and wishes of the Führer to every boy and girl, who in turn would receive instruction in all aspects of National Socialism, including some practical features of the* Sturmabteilung. *Upon reaching the age of eighteen, a Hitler boy would be encouraged to specialise in a field of his own, either within the much respected ranks of the SA or in one of the many different channels of the National Socialist Party.*

Reich Youth Leader Baldur von Schirach takes the salute at a march past of Hitler Youth in Nürnberg, 1933

Whichever way he chose to further his political interests, however, one of the fundamental principles of the Hitler Youth was to provide a secure future for the young people of Germany in an organisation where character development and training in

140

A detachment of Hitler Youth visit The Brown House, Munich, 1932

self-discipline formed the basis of all instructional programmes. To say that the Hitler Youth provided a corps of cadets for the SA would not be strictly true, although every boy chosen to enter the organisation would have as his dream the opportunity to serve as a soldier in that most élite of all military establishments.

Adolf Hitler once said, 'Youth must belong to youth', and based on that noteworthy principle, the entire strength and purpose of the Hitler Youth movement was founded. The Führer himself always maintained a very personal interest in the organisation, directing the various elements of training and setting the standards to be attained. In this way, membership rose quickly from a few hundred at the beginning to its present figure of more than one million, and in the same way that he created the SA as guardians of party ideology, so too did he create the Hitler Youth as the expression of National Socialism in the young.

A trumpet fanfare...

...and parade of drums, at the Potsdam National Youth Gathering, May 1932

Within the organisation itself, work centres on the political-cultural aspect, with youth choirs, drama groups, political indoctrination and training in military discipline. In 1932, the movement dispatched 10,000 sons and daughters of needy parents to a summer camp in the south of Germany, with three-quarters of the financial burden being found by the government.

Children's hands outstretched to greet Hitler

One of the earliest known photographs of the *Bund Deutscher Mädel*, offshoot of the Hitler Youth movement for girls, marching with banners near Berlin, 1927

The youth of Bückeberg welcome Hitler to a rally in the summer of 1935

In the same year, 115,000 members attended the National Youth Parade in Potsdam, with each division proudly carrying its own colours for more than seven hours whilst each column of uniformed youngsters marched past their Führer.

With immense courage and conviction, my colleagues and I have worked tirelessly to raise the red and white standard of the Hitler Youth movement alongside the flags of National Socialism in every town and city of Germany. With membership escalating daily, the time will soon come when every German boy and girl over the age of ten can look forward to serving their country, learning the disciplines of life and obeying the orders of their elders with pride and determination. Throughout the land, a new community of youth will be seen beating the drums of National Socialism and raising their voices in praise of its values and successes.

These will be the boys and girls who were born under the banner of Adolf Hitler, the banner they will carry all their lives and the banner for which they will eventually die. This flag that proudly bears the swastika emblem of our Führer has become the symbol of our nation's lifeblood.

Baldur von Schirach

Hitler and Reich Youth Leader Baldur von Schirach (extreme right), stop to talk to children

Youth movement parade, Bernau, May 1933

[The reader should not be deluded into thinking that Adolf Hitler was met with love and affection by the children wherever he went. On the contrary, there were numerous attempts to organise youth resistance movements, most of which were disbanded under the most awful circumstances. There was even a youth concentration camp at Neuwied, and many young people in their early teens were publicly hanged to dissuade others from following anti-Hitlerite ideology.

As a contrast to the horrors of the swastika and all it stood for, the members of the youth resistance groups adopted the white Edelweiss flower as their symbol.]

6

GERMANY MARCHES TO WAR

Whilst a time of rapid reconstruction in Germany, this was also a period of much financial stress and strain in Great Britain, resulting in a reduction of government expenditure and serious gaps in the nation's defences. Public opinion on the subject of armament was very mixed, with a good deal of pacifist and anti-militarist sentiment still lingering on from memories of First World War casualties. Since the League of Nations had been unable to check Japanese expansionism, its entire purpose and integrity left many confused thinkers, especially when the United States of America wasn't even a member of the Council of the League. Much sympathy was held for the Jewish community, and others

An historic meeting. Adolf Hitler with delegates from overseas, including Anthony Eden (third from left), discuss Germany's new foreign policy, Berlin, February 1934

Hitler delivers his welcoming speech to members of the Diplomatic Corps, New Year's Eve, Berlin, 1934

The Japanese Ambassador to Berlin (extreme left) and senior officers of the Imperial Japanese Navy visiting Hitler, 1934

who were being exiled from their own country, but the true villainy of Hitler's regime was not fully comprehended for a long time. For a number of reasons, therefore, Hitler had a head start of nearly three years before the seriousness of the situation in Germany began to be perceived overseas, and by that time, the nation had not only taken the world lead in aircraft construction, but was also building warships on a scale vastly exceeding international agreements, including submarines in secret covered dry docks.

In 1935, the British government decided it would be wise to sign a naval agreement with Germany, ignoring for the first time, the interests of her neighbouring ally, France. At a crucial stage in international affairs, there was a serious lack of understanding between London and Paris.

Hitler saw this as a weakness, and promptly occupied the Rhineland in defiance of the Treaty of Versailles. In 1936, civil war broke out in Spain, with Russia supporting the Communists, and Italy and Germany supporting General Franco. This alliance culminated a year later, in the Rome–Berlin Axis, bringing together the military might of Germany and Italy, and for the first time, really stirring up public opinion in Great Britain.

In the House of Commons, the Labour government, which had so far consistently opposed rearmament, now rapidly changed its

Hitler with the Polish Minister of Foreign Affairs, Colonel Beck

149

Meeting English veterans of the First World War trenches

views. In March 1938, Hitler marched into Austria without a single shot being fired, thereby virtually surrounding Czechoslovakia, and instilling much pressure on the Czech government. Ostensibly to defend the cause of the Sudeten Germans – settlers who had earlier crossed over the hills into north-western Czechoslovakia and now formed a substantial proportion of the population – Hitler persuaded Neville Chamberlain, the British Prime Minister, that if the frontiers could be redrawn, transferring the Sudeten district into Germany, he would cease all further territorial aspirations in Europe.

Chamberlain agreed, only to be disgusted a year later when Hitler's troops marched in and took over what still remained of Czechoslovakia.

It was clear that the situation was now becoming intensely serious. Applying the same technique as had been used in Czechoslovakia, the full blast of the Göbbels' propaganda machine was now turned towards Poland. Chamberlain attempted once again to steady the course of European politics, but the non-aggression pact signed on the 24 August 1939 between the German Foreign Minister, Joachim von Ribbentrop, and his Russian counterpart, Vyacheslav Molotov, made it all abundantly clear that there was no help to be expected from Soviet co-operation.

[The prefix 'von' in Ribbentrop's name – denoting nobility – was quite fraudulently acquired; it made its first appearance soon after January 1933, following the negotiations in his own house between Chancellor von Papen and others that resulted in Hitler becoming Chancellor of Germany.]

The Rhineland remains German! A mass gathering to mark Hitler's reannexation of the Rhineland from France, contrary to the Treaty of Versailles, March 1936

Ribbentrop is worth mentioning for a number of reasons. He was an arrogant, vain and humourless man, fanatically class-conscious, and owing everything he acquired to the favours of Adolf Hitler. He was despised by all in the Nazi Party, and was even referred to by Göring as a 'dirty little champagne-peddler' when he married Annaliese Henckel, the daughter of the largest champagne producer in Germany. His bitter rival Joseph Göbbels had no more time for him either, once remarking that 'He bought his name, and married his money, and he swindled his way into office.'

Adolf Hitler, on the other hand, would not hear a word against him, and although a latecomer to the Nazi Party, he was promoted Colonel in the much-respected SS within one year, and made personal adviser on foreign affairs a short while later. It was Ribbentrop who negotiated the Anglo-German naval agreement of

151

1935, and in August 1936, the Führer appointed him Ambassador to Great Britain. His two-year stay in London was disastrous, and deeply offended by his complete social rejection in England, he became convinced that Anglo-German antagonism was irreconcilable and henceforth always portrayed England as Germany's most dangerous of enemies.

Hitler at Labour Day celebrations, Berlin, 1 May 1934

He was also at the centre of the non-aggression pact with the Soviet Union, which paved the way for Hitler's march into Poland. Contradicting all other advisers, it was Ribbentrop alone who managed to convince Hitler that Britain would also do nothing about an attack on Poland. It was this appalling mistake that did bring Britain in direct conflict with Germany, and that cost him what little influence he still had.

He tried to cover up this disaster by pursuing an active role in the 'Final Solution', pressurising other governments to ostracise their own Jewish communities. Also of interest is the fact that, following his arrest in 1945 and subsequent trial at Nürnberg in October 1946, Ribbentrop was the first Nazi defendant to be taken to the gallows.

On 1 September 1939, the members of the German Reichstag were suddenly summoned by Hitler to a surprise meeting, in many cases being fetched by special aeroplane or motor car. They assembled at 10 o'clock to be addressed by Hitler with the news that already, at dawn, the German Wehrmacht and Luftwaffe had invaded Poland. Two days later Great Britain and France declared war on Germany, and in a broadcast specially directed at the German people, Mr Chamberlain said, 'In this war we are not fighting against you, the German people, for whom we have no bitter feeling, but against a tyrannous and forsworn regime which has betrayed not only its own people, but the entire Western civilisation, and all that we hold dear. May God defend the right.'

Hitler greets local boys on a visit to Neuschwanstein Castle, 1933

Young German girls salute the flag at their local branch of the *Bund Deutscher Mädel*

A mass gathering in front of the Frauenkirche, Nürnberg, salutes the Führer on the party's National Day, 1933

A parade of flags at the Exhibition of National Socialism in the Königsplatz, Munich, on the party's National Day, 9 November 1935

THE FÜHRER'S FOREIGN POLICY

From Adolf Hitler, published by the NSDAP Propaganda Department in 1937.

Wednesday, 17 May 1933, saw the German parliament unexpectedly summoned by the Chancellor, Adolf Hitler, to attend his declaration of foreign policy, notably at a time when the agreement on disarmament dictated a further need for the German government to make clear its position in the eyes of the world.

Hitler speaks to the nation concerning Germany's role in the world of tomorrow, at the gathering of SA units in Dortmund, May 1933

Although constantly interrupted by overwhelming applause, the Führer managed to deliver an historic speech, knowing it to be the best possible way of bringing to the world's attention the feelings of the German nation and the continuing political and economic restraints of the Versailles Treaty. Without mincing his words, he described the enormous problems of reparations, and why such liabilities were not only eroding the German economy, but also the financial progress of the entire world.

'It is because of the Versailles Accord,' the Chancellor cried

out, 'that we now find ourselves throttled beyond all sensible reason, and that the current world economic crisis continues to burden us all with its intolerable restrictions and limitations.'

In the treaty, Germany had been branded the sole guilty party in the preceding Great War, but as Adolf Hitler was quick to explain, guilt must always lie with the vanquished for it is the privilege of the victor to demand such a mandate as a prerequisite for any lasting peace.

'Such an event,' he continued, 'was all the more painful because the defeat of our great nation and the decline to that of a third-rate power, has come at a time when the League of Nations is just becoming a true international brotherhood and when any further outbreak of hostilities in Europe can only lead to the complete breakdown of international administration and the integrity of government.'

'In deciding upon a policy of complete co-operation and reassurance,' he added, 'it is the profound wish of the German government that no further misapprehension should occur, and that, furthermore, the following three points, designed to guide our own national resolve, should not in any way be seen to contradict the interests of other nations.'

Day of National Remembrance Parade, Nürnberg, 1933

157

'Firstly, the prevention of any ideology sympathetic to Communist beliefs or revolutionary intent.'

'Secondly, the immediate return of one million unemployed to the productive workforce of the nation.'

'And thirdly, the restoration of a stable government whose leadership truly warrants the trust and support of the people, and whose counsellors can play a responsible role in world affairs. National Socialism must forever remain the basic principle by which fundamental philosophies of life may be governed, and whilst we will continue to delight in the warmth of our own heritage, we must also foster a respect for the traditions of other nations. For this reason, parliament should hesitate before suggesting ideas of too rapid a pace of nationalisation; however, at the same time, it should totally repel any attempt to introduce policies contrary to our own national aspirations.'

Military attachés salute at the Day of National Socialism celebrations, Nürnberg, 1934

Thunderous applause from Reichstag members echoed the Chancellor's sentiments, and continuing in the same frank and open manner to which his people had by now grown so accustomed, he assured parliament that in pursuing a policy of disarmament and non-aggression, Germany would always

158

maintain a position of neutrality on the world's stage.

'Our nation,' he said, 'would be quite prepared to dismantle its entire military machinery if neighbouring countries would do the same. We are not considering the slightest measure of offensive intent,' he added, 'on the contrary, our policy is one of purely defensive and protective need.' The Führer further suggested that there seemed to be little reason for Germany remaining in the League of Nations, when she was constantly under such slanderous attack from all but the smallest of other overseas governments.

Hitler presides over a meeting of his military council in the Reichschancellery, Berlin, 1934. On his immediate left, seated, is Rudolf Hess, Deputy Leader of the NSDAP and last inmate of Spandau military prison, Berlin

[It was Hess who, on 10 May 1941, flew an aircraft to Britain and parachuted into the grounds of the Duke of Hamilton, in the quite incredible belief that he would be able to persuade King George VI to sack Winston Churchill, make a pact with Hitler and join forces in one vast alliance against Soviet Russia. Why he did this still baffles historians, but the most probable reason was an attempt to regain the attentions of the Führer, who by this time had largely discarded him in favour of his admirals, generals and air marshals. Doubtless he suffered from complexes of every conceivable sort, and was probably a trifle insane to boot. He was arrested upon arrival in Scotland, and remained in custody until his war trial in Nürnberg in 1945. He died, in Spandau prison, on 17 August 1987, but even that event is somewhat shrouded in mystery, as many believe it was not Hess at all.]

159

His brilliant strategy of peace, honour and goodwill, seen as yet another diplomatic masterpiece, clearly laid down the foundations of foreign policy for the new Reich. Parliament voted unanimously in favour of adopting all the principles thus laid down in the Chancellor's speech, and the stirring announcement was followed by a standing ovation and the singing of the Deutschland Lied [*the German national anthem*].

160

7

ONLY A MATTER OF TIME

The Polish campaign was not a long one. Their army, though it fought well, was vastly outmatched by the German tanks and mechanised infantry. On 17 September, however, there occurred an event quite unexpected by the outside world: Russian armies marched into Poland from the east. The battle escalated, and by the time the fighting had ceased, it was Russian troops, not German ones, that occupied most of Poland. The German people found that Hitler had paid a heavy price to secure Russia's neutrality. At the same time, the Baltic States, which had long been regarded as within the German sphere of influence, were now incorporated into the Soviet Union. These same states, after many years of bitter struggle and strife, have now shrugged off the mantle of Communism and emerged once again as proud independent nations.

Göring spending the weekend with Hitler at his home in the Obersalzberg

The *Admiral Scheer*, showing triple 11-inch gun turret

During the winter of 1939–40 the unreal war of the western front continued, with Hitler withdrawing much of his army from Poland in readiness for the next skirmish. Norway and Denmark were attacked on 9 April 1940. Belgium, Holland and Luxembourg were similarly invaded one month later, and on 22 June, the French government signed the terms of an armistice with Germany. Hitler was now to realise that his own demonic fate could no longer let him stop. He had to go on conquering until, in the end, the world would conquer him. Outside the firing range of his troops and police, all human instincts of liberty, integrity and honour were massing themselves against him. It could only be a matter of time.

This widening of the conflict into a world war soon extended the Third Reich from the Atlantic to the Caucasus, and from the Black Sea to the Baltic.

The Battle of Britain, fought in August and September 1940, afforded the first real barrier to Hitler's advances, and made it clear that an invasion of Great Britain was not possible. Throughout this period, large and intact Russian forces had been a menace on his eastern front, and on 22 June 1941, exactly a year after the armistice with France, Hitler attacked Russia. He told his ally Mussolini of his actions only when it was too late for him to make either protest or counter-proposal. Now Germany was locked into a war on two fronts, the very scene against which Hitler had vehemently warned the country in his political work *Mein Kampf.*

In October 1941, Hitler prematurely proclaimed that the Soviet Union had been struck down and would never rise again. In reality, he had seriously inderestimated the bulk of Russian military reserves and the terror of a Russian winter. German generals, including von Brauchitsch, the Commander-in-Chief, were forced to seek a withdrawal, only to find themselves, at the very thought, dismissed from all military service.

On 9 December 1941, Japan, with no declaration of war, attacked the United States of America by bombarding the naval base at Pearl Harbour in Hawaii. This brought Japan into the war alongside Germany and Italy, and the United States alongside Great Britain and the Commonwealth, the Free French and Russian forces, and all supported by various pockets of brave and gallant resistance movements throughout the Axis-occupied lands, who even to this day never lose sight of German aggression however it might be perpetrated.

Hitler now assumed personal command of all military operations himself and, refusing to listen to advice, irresponsibly

163

Launching the *Admiral Scheer*, Wilhelmshaven, 1933

disregarded unpalatable facts and rejected everything that did not fit into his preconceived picture. His neglect of the Mediterranean theatre and the Middle East, along with the complete failure of the Italians to halt the allied advance and the entry of the United States into the war, gradually pushed him onto the defensive.

From the end of 1941, the light of allied victory began to shine at the end of the tunnel, although Hitler continued to believe that implacable will and the rigid refusal to abandon positions would make up for inferior resources and the lack of sound military strategy. Convinced that his own general staff was weak and indecisive, Hitler became more and more prone to outbursts of blind hysterical fury towards his commanders when, on the other hand, he wasn't retreating into bouts of misanthropic brooding. His health too was deteriorating, largely under the impact of drugs prescribed by his quack physician, Theodor Morell, and his decline became increasingly more conspicuous by his rarer appearances in public, and his self-enforced isolation in the Wolf's Lair, his headquarters in the forests of Rastenberg, East Prussia.

By the year 1942, visible signs of the defeat of Germany were becoming apparent.

HITLER AND THE WEHRMACHT

By Lieutenant Colonel Foertsch, Nazi Party Press Office, 1935.

Adolf Hitler had himself been a volunteer soldier in the German army, who came forward to serve his country in the greatest war that any army had ever had to fight, and when that war was fought, and lost, it was he more than anyone else who realised the disastrous blunders that had been made.

Resulting from his own careful observations, he readily appreciated the steps which any new military organisation must take, particularly as to the size needed, to provide full protection along the nation's frontiers, and the necessary composition, to merit the greatest honour and respect from the nation it is tasked to defend.

Military service would be a career of dignity and devotion, but without privilege or preferential treatment for the individual, with any shortfall in numbers being made up by conscription. Despite the nation's sentiments towards pacifism and the immorality of the November Republic, Adolf Hitler soon realised that any new Wehrmacht *would quickly become a most useful tool in the framework of National Socialism.*

[Following the end of the First World War in November 1918, the name 'November Republic' was a rather sick title given to the German nation by its own people in response to the abdication of Kaiser Wilhelm II, along with the military bungling and mutinous conduct of its army. A *Wehrmacht* is literally a military machine, made up of both volunteers and conscripted men. The Versailles Treaty, amongst other things, laid down that Germany may only posses an army 100,000 strong, and all must be volunteers. This corps of dedicated professionals became known as the *Reichswehr*.]

The young officers of the postwar Reichswehr *perceived that, in Adolf Hitler, there was the one person the nation needed to restore the pride and respectability of the German military, and that a close and valuable connection would soon flourish between the founder of the NSDAP and the new armed forces.*

Early in February 1933, Adolf Hitler, by then Chancellor of Germany, called together his senior officers to a meeting in the Reichswehr *ministry to explain the basis of National Socialism and its associated politics. He assigned them all various tasks, and dictated to them exactly what he expected from them in any new* Wehrmacht *of National Socialist Germany. Details of the*

The Führer, together with the Reich Minister of War and the Army Commander-in-Chief, General Walter von Brauchitsch, discuss tactics at a military exercise at Munsterlager, August 1935

Two aircraft of the German *Luftwaffe*, in the fly-past, National Day, 1935

meeting were never made public, for Adolf Hitler felt that the German people were not yet ready to accept any new form of military ordinance, and a further two years were to elapse before the new Wehrmacht *was formally introduced to the nation.*

In his work Mein Kampf, *Hitler described the 'old gang', the army in which he had served for two years as a private soldier and later as a lance-corporal, recalling in his book, 'The army was the colossal tool of the German nation, which with utmost pride and perfection gave protection to its people like a giant umbrella, and at the same time focused hatred and delusion towards its enemies. With the signing of the Versailles Treaty it became but a fraction of its former self, not created from the hearts and minds of the people, but forced upon them by the wearisome conditions of that tragic accord.' To the Führer, it was only a small step further that transformed this small but*

167

The call to arms. The very popular parade of flags held each Party Day

Artillery pieces on display at 1935 National Day celebrations in Nürnberg

regular army into a Volksheer *[people's force], and from there into a* Wehrmacht. *The soldiers knew and understood this step, and therefore had no cause to query such decisions at the time.*

In 1933, Reichspräsident von Hindenburg honoured the Führer with the Chancellorship of Germany, a move particularly well received by the military, for they knew only too well that he alone would free the nation from the shackles of the Versailles agreement and liberate what would, once again, become the most powerful political force in the history of the nation. Everyone understood that this struggle for freedom would not be child's play, but with absolute trust and belief in the Führer, everyone knew that he would achieve this ambition. When his decision to withdraw from the League of Nations was announced, every soldier's heart beat with joy, for therein lay the first step in Germany's military reconstruction.

At the historic Remembrance Day in Potsdam in 1933, and at every festival parade thereafter, it was no surprise to see the army marching proudly alongside the SA and the founders of the National Socialist movement. In the same way that the party had neither considered a person's fortune nor his social background to be any stepping-stone to authority, so too did the new Wehrmacht become truly a people's Wehrmacht, paying little heed to a members wealth or descent.

170

'The army belongs to the people', the Führer had often said, so much so that on high days and holidays, when the military was on parade, marching orders were seldom necessary as every man's innermost feelings of pride and responsibility were more than sufficient to discipline his marching shoulder to shoulder with his comrade.

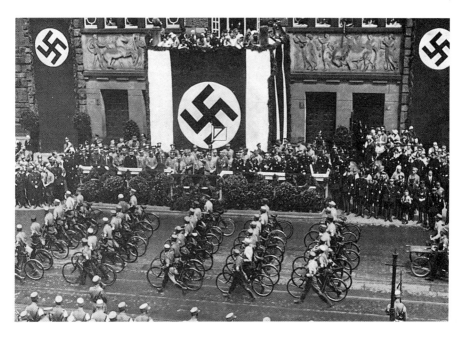

The élite corps of *Sturmabteilung* (SA) with their transport of the day march past the Führer at a party rally in Dortmund, 1933

In his Reichstag speech on 30 January 1934, Adolf Hitler announced that the NSDAP, together with the new Wehrmacht, were the two outward and visible pillars of the inward and spiritual architecture of a National Socialist Third Reich. The oath of allegiance, sworn by every man and woman in any military capacity before God, pledged total deference to the supreme commander of the Wehrmacht, and as a brave and loyal soldier, to be fully prepared to sacrifice his or her life in the cause of National Socialism. On the occasion of his own appointment, the Reichsminister of War emphasised once again the need for unquestionable faith in National Socialism as the basis for discipline in military service, and the reality that a new-found bond between the Führer and his Wehrmacht was in

171

The military parade at the National Party Day celebrations in Nürnberg in 1935 was the first time that the world saw what was going on in Germany. Here detachments of naval ratings march past the Führer. Grand Admiral Räder, the Naval Commander-in-Chief, is seen at his left side

172

Germany's rearmament programme provided for tanks at a very early date. Here the PzKpw Panzer I is seen on exercise in October 1935

every way similar to the affinity already seen to be established between the Führer and any farm labourer or political agitator. In one breath, each and every man making this oath could claim the Führer as his own, knowing full well that he too had come from country folk, to fight in the trenches and serve his country throughout the Great War. Old comrades who had fought with the Führer loved to meet him and talk of past glories and heroic deeds, and knowing him to be truly the bravest of soldiers at heart, now understood his claim of every right to demand the same devotion to others. Through his own experiences and close contact with the enemy, the Führer readily understood the needs and tortures that governed the lives of fighting men.

In this way, Führer and Wehrmacht, Wehrmacht and nation, nation and Führer became wholly bound by oath and covenant to serve, for the common good, a free, united and ever powerful National Socialist Germany.

Hitler's visit to the fleet, Kiel, May 1934

Heavy artillery on display at the 1935 National Day parade

174

The newly launched communications vessel *Aviso Grille*, used by Hitler during his visits to the German navy

Rommel's defeat at El Alamein and his subsequent loss of North Africa to the allies was matched in January 1943 by another German disaster at Stalingrad, where General von Paulus and the 6th Army were completely cut off and forced to surrender to the Russian command. Six months later, Mussolini's regime in Italy collapsed, resulting in an armistice being signed in September 1943 between the Italian government and the allies. The invasion of Normandy followed on 6 June 1944, and soon a million allied troops were driving the Germans eastwards, whilst from the other direction Soviet forces were now advancing relentlessly on Prussian soil. An all-out mobilisation of the German war effort under the Reichsminister for Armaments and Production, Albert Speer, did for a while managed to slow down allied advances on some fronts.

(Incidentally, at Russia's insistence, Albert Speer was one of a very few who did serve a full 20-year term in Spandau prison after the war. He was released in 1966, and died in a London hospital on 1 September 1981, on a private visit to the United Kingdom.)

Coastal motor torpedo boat *S5*, designed to protect German ports along the coasts of France

Despite the equally energetic propaganda efforts of Joseph Göbbels to rouse the fighting spirit of the German people, it became increasingly obvious that the Third Reich simply lacked the resources for the struggle against a world alliance that Hitler himself had provoked. Allied bombing by this time was having

176

such a telling effect on German industry and the morale of the people that a small group of senior officers, assisted by the internal German resistance movement, decided to assassinate Adolf Hitler, hoping thereby to pave the way for a negotiated peace settlement that would save Germany from total destruction. The Valkyrie Plan, as it was called, was the brainchild of Colonel Claus von Stauffenberg, very much a member of the German aristocracy, who together with his colleagues in the plot, was convinced that the war was lost and that further military action would drag both Hitler and the Fatherland deeper into the tomb. As Chief of Staff to General Friedrich Fromm, commander of all German reserve units, von Stauffenberg often had official reason for visiting Hitler's headquarters. He was chosen to carry out the assassination since he was the only conspirator who could attend Hitler's staff conferences without being searched. It was arranged that he would kill Hitler, together with Göring and Himmler, at Berchtesgaden on 2 July 1944, but as Göring and Himmler didn't turn up, the attempt was postponed. The second attempt, on 15 July, was also postponed at the very last minute because Hitler himself became indisposed. Von Stauffenberg now resolved to eliminate Hitler at the next opportunity, even if the others were absent, as the allies were advancing fast, lessening with every passing day any hope of a compromise peace.

On 20 July, von Stauffenberg attended a meeting at the Wolf's Lair, carrying a bomb in his briefcase. It was primed to explode ten minutes after being carefully placed unobtrusively against the leg of the table in the map room, where Hitler always stood whilst discussing the military situation. As previously arranged, von Stauffenberg was called away to answer the telephone, but instead, he made his way to his car through two checkpoints, and even succeeded in returning to Berlin by aeroplane, convinced, of course, that Hitler was dead.

Unfortunately, one of the officers present unwittingly moved the briefcase as it was a little in the way, thereby saving the Führer's life and extending the war a further ten months. Hitler was very badly shaken, and four other officers were killed, but von Stauffenberg's fellow conspirators in Berlin made only a half-hearted attempt to fully consummate the *coup d'état*, being uncertain whether Hitler was alive or not. Moreover, von Stauffenberg's associate at Rastenberg failed in his prime task of sabotaging the communications centre, thus enabling the Führer both to learn what was happening in Berlin, and to broadcast to the nation the news that he had survived the assasination attempt.

In the subsequent confusion, Fromm quickly arrested von Stauffenberg and had him shot in the War Ministry courtyard, lit up by the lights of an army lorry. The other mastermind in the plot, General Ludwig Beck, was persuaded to commit suicide rather than be captured. He twice unsuccessfully attempted to blow his brains out with a pistol, finally being finished off by a shot in the neck from his own sergeant. *(It is very interesting to note that, had this attempt on Hitler's life succeeded, and it very nearly did, General von Beck would have taken Hitler's place as Head of State.)*

Hitler pays a visit to the old battleship *Schleswig-Holstein*, during a visit to Hamburg, May 1936
(The *Schleswig-Holstein* and her sister ship, the *Schlesien*, were the only capital ships remaining from the days of the First World War. The *Schleswig-Holstein* was used solely as a gunnery training ship in the period of rearmament, and did not see active service again, whereas the *Schlesien* played quite a successful role during the Second World War, finally sinking off the port of Swinemünde, having struck mines, only days from the end of hostilities.)

Fromm's cowardly betrayal was in fact to no avail. On the next day he too was arrested at the orders of Himmler, sentenced to death, and executed by firing-squad. The full force of Hitler's revenge, expressed through the machinery of Himmler and the SS, swept away not only those actively connected with the plot, but all those who might have been remotely associated with it. It is calculated that in a lengthy series of cruel and brutal executions, more than 5,000 people lost their lives, and even more finished up in concentration camps. The final result of the Valkyrie Plan was that almost all the people who might conceivably have formed the leadership of a German government after Hitler, had now been eliminated by execution squads. Furthermore, Hitler and the Nazi leaders were now more brutal, more mad and certainly more determined to fight to utter destruction than ever before. The months from August 1944 to May 1945 were months of despair for the German population. If they managed to escape the perpetual allied bombing, then they had to contend with ever-increasing police terror from within their own people.

As the Soviet army approached Berlin, and the allies poised to cross the river Elbe on 19 March 1945, Adolf Hitler ordered the complete destruction of all remaining German industry,

Hitler attending the commissioning of *U7*, in September 1935. By the end of that year, Dönitz, the U-boat fleet commander, had a fleet of nine U-boats – called the Weddingen flotilla, after Otto Weddingen, the most successful U-boat commander of the First World War

179

communications and transport systems. He was quite resolved that if he did not survive, then Germany too must be destroyed. The same nihilism and passion for destruction which had led to the extermination of six million Jews in death camps, along with the biological cleansing of 'sub-human' Slavs and others in his 'Final Solution', were finally turned on his own people. On 29 April 1945, he married his mistress, Eva Braun, and dictated his final political testament with the same monotonous and obsessive fixation that had guided him throughout his monstrous career.

Hitler often visited the graves of 'fallen martyrs' in the cemetery of Luisenstadt, Berlin. This time he is accompanied by the chief of propaganda, Dr Joseph Göbbels

'Above all,' he said, 'I charge the leaders of this nation, and those under them, to the scrupulous observance of racial supremacy, and to the merciless opposition of the universal poison, international Jewry.'

On the following day, 30 April 1945, Hitler committed suicide by shooting himself through the mouth with a revolver. His body was carried into the garden of the Reichschancellery by his personal aides, covered with petrol and, along with that of Eva Braun, burned to charred ashes.

With his death there remained nothing of the great Germanic nation and the tyrannical power structure and ideological systems that had devastated the continent of Europe during the 12 years of his totalitarian rule.

THE FÜHRER AND HIS PRIVATE LIFE

An account by SS Oberstandführer Wilhelm Bücher.

Hitler's home in Berchtesgaden, in the mountains of the Obersalzberg

Only someone so totally devoted to a nation and its politics as the Führer, Adolf Hitler, could sacrifice so much of his private life for his public duties, to the extent that even when managing to escape to his mountain retreat in the Obersalzberg or his seaside haven by the Baltic, the sheer volume of work never ceases to surround him.

With telephone calls, telegrams, letters and messages continually pressing on his daily life, the Führer knows in his heart that there can be no escape from the path he has chosen, the path of Germany and its people.

Adolf Hitler always retires to bed late, only to rise again at the break of day, ready to face fresh problems in the field of foreign affairs or in the planning of new financial negotiations. However, above all else, it is always the question of feeding his people and the education of its youth that fills most of his time, with hardly a day going past without his chairing a meeting in some way connected with the welfare of the nation, its military

181

security or its heritage and culture.

Every day begins and ends with the Führer seated at his desk, and even when he does manage to slip away for a few days' peace and quiet, it is invariably to find the time to review ministerial matters or prepare speeches for future council. He remains in constant touch with his Reich leaders even whilst flying, to the extent that his private and public lives have become virtually one and the same thing, a life of absolute love and devotion for his country. Mention of his private life really means that his public life has temporarily assumed more comfortable surroundings.

Hitler celebrates his birthday on a flight to Berlin, 20 April 1932

Despite his complete attachment to his work, he always looks forward to a few moments when he can enjoy his passion for the arts and sciences. At the end of a full day, his most pleasurable desire is to be in the company of beautiful music, in fact many important matters of state have had their beginnings in the tranquil atmosphere of an opera or a concert. When entertaining guests, he is never happier than when in the company of leading musicians, who delight in playing their best for the Führer or joining him in his rich and intellectual discussions on musical or dramatic affairs.

Close behind this love of music is his special interest in films,

182

Girls greeting Hitler
on his visit to their school

nowadays the youngest member in the world of artistic achievement. A projector installed in the great hall of the Reichschancellery allows the Führer to see events almost as they happen, both in Germany and around the globe, and in between his many engagements, he often invites visitors to join him for lunch in order to discuss the latest events just recorded on film. In this way, Adolf Hitler has brought together men from every walk of life, officers, scientists, bankers, businessmen, party leaders and wartime comrades, in order to dine with him and freely exchange their knowledge and ideas. Most weekends see the Führer trying hard to find the time to visit his people, gauge at first hand their moods and impressions, and personally inspect projects that he has initiated. It is always a moving experience for those fortunate enough to witness the enormous love shown by the people for their Führer.

Hitler takes a break
during a campaign drive,
summer 1932

183

Hitler relaxing in the Harz mountains in October 1934

He often welcomed children on the balcony of his house

184

During a rare opportunity to enjoy some skiing, Hitler greets every passer-by

His favourite haunts are his home at Berchtesgaden in the Obersalzberg, and one or two hiding-places on the shores of the Baltic sea, which he usually visits when only a short break permits. Mornings are always especially busy, with the Führer working hard to complete the day's programme in plenty of time to allow him the opportunity for an afternoon drive through the countryside. Best loved of his excursions from Berchtesgaden are to Königsee, the jewel of the German Alps, or to the small hillside tavern at Hochlenzer. He often visits the nearby home of Reichsführer Hermann Göring, who also shares with the Führer the love of archery. During these visits to the country, the Führer always insists on stopping in some of the picturesque villages or particular spots of scenic beauty, where he invariably meets other people out to enjoy themselves. Whenever possible, he invites them to join him in a stroll or partake of his picnic. However, more than for any other reason, the purpose of having his home in the mountains of Obersalzberg is because of the spectacular view over the country that he loves so much. It is also whilst staying in Berchtesgaden that Adolf Hitler feels particularly close to his people, for they come from all over Germany to visit him, and he never fails to speak to each and every one.

185

The living-room and (below) the dining-area of Hitler's house in Berchtesgaden, Obersalzberg. [*Note the saluting soldier on the hanging lamp.*]

In the evenings he enjoys a walk through the beechwoods behind the sand dunes, or in the pine forests of the mountains, where he is often accompanied by children, who press forward to hold his hand and relate adventures of their lives. Whenever he can, he invites visitors to his home to join him for lunch or tea, a time of much pleasure and laughter, and always a memorable occasion for the lucky few.

Accompanied by his Reichsminister for Propaganda, Joseph Göbbels (on his immediate left), Hitler enjoys entertaining guests at his home in Berchtesgaden

As evening gives way to night, Adolf Hitler is seen once again hard at work receiving telephone calls from his Reich leaders or dealing with correspondence and telegrams. It is also at this time that he usually manages to study all those papers and documents for which there was no opportunity in Berlin. He is always the last to retire at night and the first to rise in the morning, taking a quick glance at the newspapers before a working breakfast and another full day ahead.

His own guests at Berchtesgaden are always made most welcome, among them perhaps Hermann Göring, Joseph Göbbels and General Inspector of Reichsautobahn Dr Fritz Todt are the most frequent.

187

Last but not least, the animals too find a place in the warm heart of the Führer. He has great affection for his pack of wolfhounds, and loves to admire the many birds that come to feed from the numerous trays around his garden.

Nevertheless, his visits to mountain or coastal retreat are always too short and are invariably followed by a hasty return to Berlin and ever more pressing affairs of state. In the same way that the mountains have stood for more than a thousand years, so too will his devotion to Germany and its people stand for more than a thousand years to come.

With Dr Joseph Göbbels on his left, Reichsführer Hermann Göring on his right, and other senior Reichsministers, Hitler attends a performance by the Berlin Philharmonic Orchestra under their Director, Wilhelm Furtwängler
[Wilhelm Furtwängler was one of the finest conductors of this century. He succeeded Richard Strauss as chief conductor of the Berlin Opera Company, and in 1922 was appointed director of the Berlin Philharmonic, a position he held until the end of the Second World War. He enjoyed a rather stormy relationship with Adolf Hitler, largely due to his support of certain composers denounced by Nazi propaganda as 'musical degenerates'. Nevertheless, what is interesting is that his brilliant direction of the Berlin Philharmonic Orchestra and his mutually beneficial accommodation with Nazi authorities greatly helped to cover up the degradation of almost all other art forms under the Third Reich.]

Hundreds of well-wishers greeting Hitler outside his home in the Obersalzberg, on the occasion of his 50th birthday, April 1939

CONCLUSION

Germany was left in industrial and administrative chaos. There was very little food, very few resources and virtually no money in the land. The four allied powers had already drawn up plans for the administration of Germany after the war, in the Yalta accord of December 1944. Britain, Russia, the United States and France would each have a zone of occupation, with the United States also having the port district of Bremen in order to receive supplies by sea. Britain not only had the facilities at Cuxhaven, through which my mother and I arrived in 1946, but also the ports along the Dutch coast with rail connections to all the military districts of the British Zone. Russia and France both had common borders with their zones of occupation, which facilitated direct supply.

Within a few years of the war ending, the zones of the Western powers had amalgamated to form the Federal Republic of West Germany, with Dr Konrad Adenauer as Chancellor and a seat of government established in the city of Bonn. Berlin, the ancestral capital of Germany, although lying entirely within the Russian Zone, was occupied by all four allied powers, sectors of the Western Alliance eventually amalgamating to form West Berlin, whilst the Soviet sector became known as East Berlin. Until recently, the Berlin Wall stood as a stark reminder of Communist overbearing, separating not only West from East, but Freedom from Oppression.

Today we are witnessing, once again, dramatic changes in central Europe, perhaps the most dramatic since the fall of the Third Reich. The removal of the Berlin Wall and a new-found democracy in East Germany have resulted once again in a single German nation. I am only sorry that my father, who strove for many years to build up the belief in a united Germany, was not able to see it happen. Let us not, however, be blind to the aspirations of many who, with the excitement of reunification and the profits to be made, have already had dreams of another Reich, and a return to German supremacy in the world.

Not long before my father retired from Control Commission service, he held a large farewell party for all the many friends, both English and German, he had made in his 14 years in Germany. 'I will never forget,' he told me, 'the words of one elderly gentleman as he said goodbye: "You know, Colonel, twice we have lost the war, next time we really must win!"'

Adolf Hitler